KRISTI MCLELLAND

Jesus & Women

for teen girls

Lifeway Press®
Brentwood, Tennessee

Published by Lifeway Press®
© 2023 Kristi McLelland

ISBN: 978-1-0877-7455-8
Item: 005839547
Dewey decimal classification: 248.83
Subject heading: RELIGION / Christian Ministry / Youth

To order additional copies of this resource, write Lifeway Resources Customer Service; 200 Powell Place, Suite 100; Brentwood, TN 37027;
Fax order to 615.251.5933; call toll-free 800.458.2772; email orderentry@lifeway.com; or order online at www.lifeway.com.

Printed in the United States of America.

Student Ministry Publishing
Lifeway Resources
200 Powell Place, Suite 100
Brentwood, TN 37027

EDITORIAL TEAM, LIFEWAY GIRLS BIBLE STUDIES

Ben Trueblood
Director, Lifeway Students

John Paul Basham
Manager

Karen Daniel
Team Leader

Amanda Mejias
Content Editor

April-Lyn Caouette
Production Editor

**Shiloh Stufflebeam
Amy Lyon**
Graphic Designers

EDITORIAL TEAM, LIFEWAY WOMEN BIBLE STUDIES

Becky Loyd
Director, Adult Ministry

Michelle Hicks
Manager, Adult Ministry Short Term Bible Studies

Sarah Doss
Content Editor

Erin Franklin
Production Editor

Lauren Ervin
Graphic Designer

Micah Kandros Design
Cover Designer

Table of Contents

ABOUT THE AUTHOR

KRISTI MCLELLAND is a speaker, teacher, and college professor. Since completing her Masters of Arts in Christian Education at Dallas Theological Seminary, she has dedicated her life to discipleship, teaching people how to study the Bible for themselves and writing about how God is better than we ever knew, explaining the Bible through a Middle Eastern lens. Her great desire for people to truly experience the love of God birthed a ministry in which she leads biblical study trips to Israel, Turkey, Greece, and Italy.

For more information about Kristi and what she's up to, visit: NewLensBiblicalStudies.com.

INTRODUCTION

"A BIBLE WITH ITS JEWISHNESS WRUNG OUT OF IT IS NO BIBLE. A CHRIST WITH HIS JEWISHNESS OBSCURED IS NO CHRIST AT ALL." [1]
—DR. RUSSELL MOORE

Every adventure begins in a moment, and the best ones come to us. In 2007. an adventure found me. The Lord opened the door for me to go study the Bible in Egypt and Israel.

At the time, I was teaching the Bible in the Biblical Studies department at Williamson College. I went to the Middle East in a spirit of professional development, just to learn. But God had other plans—much better plans.

In Israel, I was amazed to see how different the Middle Eastern culture was and is from our Western culture. I started noticing how I was approaching the Bible as a Westerner, seeing it with Western eyes and asking Western questions of the biblical text. In Israel I learned the Bible through a cultural lens, the Middle Eastern lens.

In these early days of my Middle Eastern study, God totally and thoroughly wrecked me in the best of ways. He completely transformed me.

Learning the Bible in its original historical, cultural, linguistic, and geographic context allowed me to get to know Jesus in *His* Jewish world. I didn't just fly over to Israel; it felt almost as if I went back in time to learn about the first-century world of the Bible, the world Jesus lived in two thousand years ago.

"WE HAVE FORGOTTEN THAT WE READ THE BIBLE AS FOREIGNERS, AS VISITORS WHO HAVE TRAVELED NOT ONLY TO A NEW GEOGRAPHY BUT A NEW CENTURY. WE ARE LITERARY TOURISTS WHO ARE DEEPLY IN NEED OF A GUIDE." [2]
—GARY M. BURGE

You may be wondering about the meaning behind the cover of our study. The vessel pictured there is a tear jar, an archaeological artifact dating back to the first or second century AD. It was uncovered in Israel where one of my professors gave it to me as a gift.

This tear jar most likely belonged to an ancient Jewish woman, maybe even in the lifetime of Jesus's earthly ministry. In the ancient Near East, Jewish women collected their tears in a jar like this and poured them out to God in worship as a sign of faith, embodying God's message in Psalm 56:8, where He says He keeps our tears in a bottle. I look at the tear jar often and wonder what the original owner's story might have looked like—what she experienced, her highs and lows. I wonder where she kept her jar and how often she pulled it out to collect her tears before the Lord.

To me, the tear jar represents some of what a woman in Jesus's first-century world would have experienced. She was not always valued by society; she was often marginalized. Yet God saw her grief and her struggle. He encouraged her to bring her pain to Him in worship and prayer. Then, through Jesus, He worked to restore the woman and show her His redemptive purposes in her life. He valued her; He lifted her up out of shame. He set her on the path to life. And He desires to do the same for you and for me, as followers of Christ.

I went to Israel and learned that God is *better* than I ever knew.

This understanding of who God is has changed me, and it's changing me still. I believe it will do the same for you. My time in Israel marked my life and shifted its direction entirely. I've been taking teams to Israel for Bible study trips since 2007. The gift given to me has become my gift to give others. My hope is for this study to be that gift to you.

The Bible was primarily written by Middle Easterners in a Middle Eastern context. Deeper insight into the Middle Eastern culture and historical context of the time in which the Bible was written will greatly add to our understanding of what the biblical authors meant by what they wrote and what the people described in the Bible did.

One of the major differences between Western and Eastern culture is *how* we teach and *how* we learn. We, in the West, are more of a Greco-Roman culture.

We prize literature. We read sitting at desks, study with books in our hands, take notes, fill in the answers, and finish our workbooks.

Teaching and learning are different in the Middle East—they're different now, and they were different for Jesus in His time on earth. Middle Eastern teaching is visual; a rabbi teaches on the go. When Jesus taught, He could usually see the object of His lessons, and His disciples could see it too. This teaching style wasn't just philosophical. It was not "up there;" it was "down here."

Jesus's style wasn't to provide a syllabus or a workbook. He was more likely to walk through a field of mustard plants while sharing a parable about how the kingdom of God is like a mustard seed.

In the Middle Eastern style of learning, the student wants to stay very close to the rabbi so as not to lose any of their rabbi's words. And the student never knows when or where the rabbi will begin teaching! In the Middle Eastern way, students learn through discovery rather than the acquisition of knowledge. This is how a rabbi teaches—they guide you into discovery. And this is how I want to guide you through our eight weeks together.

We are going to strive to view the Bible through a Middle Eastern lens and, at the same time, study a few Bible passages in a traditionally Jewish way, the way rabbis still teach the children in Israel today. We will walk into discoveries together rather than simply being taught the content or lesson.

This eight-week feast is my attempt to set a biblical table around which we can come together and discover Jesus's heart for women in His first-century world. At this table, we take off our Western lenses and put on our Middle Eastern lenses. I'll continue to share bits and pieces along the way to guide you in shaping your Middle Eastern lens.

I'm so honored and expectant to share in this eight-week biblical feast with you. In some ancient way, the Lord saw this for us before the foundations of the world were ever even laid. He's drawing us to this table, and He will do the feeding. Posture yourself to receive.

All the best,

Kristi V. McClelland

HOW TO USE THIS STUDY

In our time together, we're going to study God's Word in a way that might seem a bit different from what you've experienced in the past. As I mentioned in the introduction, we are going to strive to view the Bible through a Middle Eastern lens and, at the same time, study a few Bible passages in a traditionally Jewish way—the way the rabbis would have taught the Bible to Jesus, and the way some rabbis still teach the children in Israel today.

With that in mind, let's discuss a bit of the framework for our study:

We approach the Scriptures as children expecting to be fed by our Father.

It can be easy to sit down with our Bibles and think something like, *okay, let me figure out some application from the passage I'm reading today.* I have good news for you—we are not spiritual orphans. We have a gracious heavenly Father who feeds us to the full with His Word; He gives abundantly. As we read the Word, we do our part by being open to what God will teach us. We posture ourselves to obey and to be gratefully fed by the Living God through His Word and by the power of His Spirit. But ultimately, God is in charge of feeding us.

We're not looking for the "right" answer.

Though it may sound strange to our Western ears, in Judaism, the student with good questions is better than the student with all of the right answers. We never just read the Bible; we interact with it, asking questions of the text. We want to know what a text teaches us about God before we ask what it teaches us about ourselves. In our time together, we're going to focus on interacting with the biblical text in community, and we're going to learn to be okay with questions that cannot be easily answered and even questions that may leave us scratching our heads.

We want God's Word to become a part of who we are.

The Middle Eastern way of learning involves more of an oral teaching tradition, rather than the more formal learning style of our Western world. In our study together, we want these concepts in God's Word to get into our hearts and minds so much that they become a part of who we are, changing the way we see God and interact with the world. You'll notice we will revisit some of the same concepts each week. The study is designed this way on purpose. By the end of our time together, I hope these biblical concepts are so clear and familiar they are almost second nature to you.

Learning will be done inside community.

In the Middle Eastern, learning is very communal. Here's what I mean: in a Middle Eastern context, it would be common to see rabbis teaching students as they walk down the road. This teaching tradition places significant value on students discussing an issue with one another. Rabbis often instruct their students to "go first" and discuss what they believe about a teaching before the teacher explains the concept to them. We're going to adopt some of those ideas in our time together. In many cases, I'll "go first" in our feast teaching times. But you'll notice group times that I've crafted especially for you to use as you *yeshiva*, or discuss biblical texts together, after we begin unpacking them in our video teaching times.

Note that terms in the text marked with *this style* are explained in further detail in the glossary on pages 142–151.

BEFORE YOU GET STARTED, MAKE SURE YOU DOWNLOAD THE TEACHING VIDEO BUNDLE AT LIFEWAY.COM/JESUSANDWOMEN. SCAN THIS QR CODE TO GET STARTED.

Throughout our sessions together, you'll find these sections:

WITH YOUR GROUP

- The **FEAST** section includes questions to begin your time together and a space to take notes as you watch the video teaching as a group.

- The **YESHIVA** section includes questions for your small group to explore together. We'll dive into further insight on a topic we discussed in our feast teaching times.

ON YOUR OWN

- In the **LOOK** section, we'll highlight a Middle Eastern insight or cultural emphasis more in-depth to further your understanding of Jesus's first-century world.

- In the **LEARN** section, we'll take a passage of Scripture and consider it through a Middle Eastern lens.

- In the **LIVE** section, we'll take some time to help you apply the concepts you're learning to your own life.

The **LOOK, LEARN,** and **LIVE** sections are for your personal study time. Instead of labeling them by days of study, we've labeled them by sections. Feel free to complete each between our weekly group times as you see fit throughout the week.

Are you ready? Let's go!

Session One

MEETING THE MIDDLE EASTERN JESUS

{ THE FEAST }

For me, the best meal is one I don't have to cook. When we come to the Word of God, that's absolutely true for all of us—God prepares this feast for us. We come to this moment and to this table believing the Living God will feed us. We are not orphans, and we are not fatherless. We don't have to scrounge, strive, or strain to feed ourselves the Word of God. We can simply, yet profoundly, posture ourselves to receive the feast the Lord has prepared for us—for you.

BEGIN

As we begin our feast, take a few moments to answer the following questions before you watch the video teaching.

How would you describe the world's view of a woman?

Do you think God's view of women is similar or different? Explain why you think that way.

Are you familiar with any stories of Jesus interacting with women in Scripture? If so, which story are you hoping we learn more about?

What do you think would have made Jesus seem different to the people of His day?

What are you asking the Lord to do in your life through this eight-session feast?

Use the space on the following page or the blank pages at the back of this book during our feast teaching time to add your own notes as you watch.

THE TEACHING SESSION BUNDLE IS AVAILABLE FOR PURCHASE AT LIFEWAY.COM/JESUSANDWOMEN

WESTERN LENS	MIDDLE EASTERN LENS
Form	Function
How? *How did it happen?*	Why? *Why would God do that?*
Understand → Believe	Believe → Understand
Law, Rule, Principle	Story, Narrative
What does it teach me about *me*?	What does it teach me about *God*?
Dig deep, get down in it . . . *(Analysis—pick it apart)*	Read through it . . . *(Synthesis—bring it together)*
Study to acquire *knowledge*	Posture to be *fed*

{ YESHIVA }

As we discussed in our first "biblical feast" together, Middle Easterners most often learn and cultivate spiritual growth within the context of community and group conversation. With this cultural difference in mind, each week we're going to practice *yeshiva* together—what we might call "workshopping" or "brainstorming" around a topic in our Western culture—dialoging openly about a biblical concept and walking together as a community with Jesus as our rabbi. Discuss the following questions with your group.

Yeshiva

Stemming from the Hebrew verb that means "to dwell," yeshiva occurred when students would discuss or debate questions or comments from a teacher.[1] This means a community would determine the validity of a biblical teaching through yeshiva.

What did you just *hear* or *see* in our feast together that you want to remember?

How does the concept of *eating* the Word of God differ from *reading* the Word of God?

Describe your posture towards God's Word. Do you want to see that posture change in any way? If so, explain why.

Have you ever thought about the differences between reading the Bible through our Western lens versus a Middle Eastern lens? Why do you think it's important to see the differences?

We're going to engage with the Western versus Middle Eastern lens chart (p. 13) during each of our eight feasts together. This session isn't going to cover the chart exhaustively, but I do want us to familiarize ourselves with two ways our culture as modern Westerners differs from that of the ancient biblical world.

Like the story of the dentist in Israel that was shared in the video, what is the difference between form and function?

The second part of the chart highlights the differences between the questions asked. Oftentimes when we read the Bible, we ask the question, *What does this teach me about me?* We go in and down. But in the Middle East, they read the Scriptures and they ask a different question. They ask, *What does this teach me about God, about who He is and what He's like?* This kind of question lifts us up, gets our gaze focused outward on Him.

If you stare at yourself for too long, you'll get depressed. But staring at God will change your life. My prayer is that through this feast we will stare at God, who sees our lives through His perspective, through who He is.

What are the dangers of approaching Scripture with a "me" focus?

As we make our way through our first feast, as we are learning a little bit better to take off our Western glasses and to put our Middle Eastern glasses on, I want you to turn now in your Bibles to the final chapter of the final book of the Old Testament.

READ MALACHI 4:2.

Malachi was the last writing prophet of the Old Testament. These would be some of the last words that the Jewish people would hear from God before heading into the four hundred years of the intertestamental period.

> Do you think the Israelites remembered what Malachi said? Based on the verse you read, what do you think they would be looking for in a Messiah?

I can imagine the Jewish people having conversations during that intertestamental period asking things like: "When Messiah comes, what kind of things will He be saying, what kind of things will He be doing? How will we recognize Him?" But because they are a people of remembrance and a people of the Scripture, they'd go back to this verse in Malachi 4:2, and they say, "Ah, that's right. When the Son of Righteousness comes, when Messiah comes, we will know it because He will have healing in His wings."

This was their hope. Next session, we are going to fast forward to the New Testament to see how one woman would not only know Malachi 4:2, but experience "healing in His wings" firsthand.

> Take a look at Psalm 63:7 below, then read it aloud as a group together before heading into the final section of your group time.

Because you are my help, I sing in the shadow of your wings.

PSALM 63:7

LIVING LIKE A RIVER, NOT A LAKE

I've been taking team members to the Jordan River for eleven years now. The Jordan River flows from the Sea of Galilee into the Dead Sea. The water moves, flows—it's living water, *mayim chayim*.[2] I've also floated in the Dead Sea. The water in the Dead Sea is still, motionless—it's dead water.

As a college professor, I tell my students all the time, "You haven't learned a thing when you've seen it. You haven't learned a thing when you've heard it. You haven't learned a thing when you have seen and heard it. You've learned a thing when you can give it away." We want the Word of God to travel through us to others, moving freely as a river would. We are not supposed to hold what God is teaching us to ourselves, motionless like the Dead Sea.

The things the Lord reveals to you—what He feeds you in this feast—are meant to travel through you to others. We want to live like rivers, not lakes.

Consider the following questions and record your answers below:
How can this feast travel through you this week?

Who needs to hear the truths you've learned at this week's feast?

Who can you be a river for this week?

Session Two

TAKE HEART, DAUGHTER

THE FEAST

As we prepare to watch our second video teaching together, we are getting ready to pull up our chairs for Session Two of this biblical feast. I call our study times together "feasts" because we don't so much read the Word of God as eat it. We take it in—we let it do its work in us.

BEGIN

As we begin our feast, take a few moments to answer the following questions before you watch the video teaching.

What have you been thinking about since last week's feast?

Who did you live like a river toward last week by sharing what you learned at the feast?

How did that conversation go? How did your time together challenge you or confirm what you've been learning?

Use the following space or the blank pages at the back of this book during our feast teaching time to add your own notes as you watch.

THE TEACHING SESSION BUNDLE IS AVAILABLE FOR PURCHASE AT LIFEWAY.COM/JESUSANDWOMEN

WESTERN LENS	MIDDLE EASTERN LENS
Form	Function
How? *How did it happen?*	Why? *Why would God do that?*
Understand → Believe	Believe → Understand
Law, Rule, Principle	Story, Narrative
What does it teach me about *me*?	What does it teach me about *God*?
Dig deep, get down in it . . . *(Analysis—pick it apart)*	Read through it . . . *(Synthesis—bring it together)*
Study to acquire *knowledge*	Posture to be *fed*

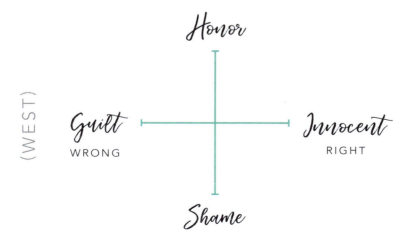

(MIDDLE EAST)

Honor

(WEST)

Guilt
WRONG

Innocent
RIGHT

Shame

{ YESHIVA }

After hearing the story of Matthew 9 in our feast, how does that Scripture feel different when you read it now?

You might be using your smartphone Bible app, but if you have a physical Bible close by, I want you to get it. Find the page that separates the Old Testament from the New Testament; it can be found right between Malachi and Matthew.

Most likely, you will find a blank white page between the two testaments. This might make you think that not a lot happened during that blank page in history, but a lot did happen! We're going to get to that next week when we come together. But these words are important for us, and they were very important for the Jewish people—these words are the last words the living God gave the Israelite people before they entered into the time period known as the "intertestamental period." That little white page in your Bibles between Malachi and Matthew covers four hundred years. Sometimes scholars and theologians have called the intertestamental period "the silent years." That can be a little bit misleading, as if the living God just took a vacation for four hundred years and stopped speaking or doing anything. That isn't the case at all.

What we mean by "the silent years" is that there was no writing prophet of Israel (like Malachi) at that time. So Malachi serves as our last writing prophet of the Old Testament, and he serves as that for the Jewish people. The Jewish people look at Malachi 4 as the last words the living God gave His people before they headed into the four hundred years of the intertestamental period.

Think about someone you really love who you haven't gotten to talk to in a long time. Maybe it's a friend who lives far away or a family member who passed away. Do you remember the last thing you talked about with that person? Write down what they said to you.

Why do you think you remember those words?

If you remember your loved one's words, don't you think the Jewish people remembered the words of Malachi? The last words they'd hear from God for four hundred years? Those words in Malachi 4 would be their messianic hope, an expectation of how they would recognize the Messiah when He came onto the scene.

For four hundred years, the Jewish people had been walking around with Malachi 4:2 in their spirits: *When the Sun of Righteousness comes, part of how we will recognize Him is He will have healing in His wings.*

What do you think people thought about Jesus? What about Him probably stood out to those watching?

READ MATTHEW 9:18-22.

In Matthew 9, we are introduced to a woman. The Bible tells us that she has had an "issue of blood" for twelve years. And there is apparently something about Jesus that makes this woman believe that just maybe He is the Messiah—the One who Malachi had talked about in the Scriptures, four hundred years previously.

So as Jesus is making His way through the crowds, this woman shows up. A woman who is not supposed to touch other people, because if she does, she will make them unclean.

What did this woman need from Jesus?

Even though I don't know for sure, I believe with all of my heart that this woman knew Malachi 4:2. Because the Bible says that she reached out and grabbed something on Jesus.

What did she grab? His wing.

According to Malachi, healing would be found in the Messiah's wing. This woman's reaching out and grabbing hold of a holy rabbi of Israel—this is bravery. This is courage. This is a woman taking the living God at His Word and demonstrating faith in her day and time. And what I love about the Bible is it says that when she grabbed a hold of His *kanaf*, His wing, and she was healed. She found healing in the wing of the Son of Righteousness.

What is the hurt or pain inside of you that you need healing from?

Do you believe that Jesus has the power to heal you? Why or why not?

What would it look like for you to show courage and ask God to heal you today?

Part of what I love about this story is that Jesus doesn't have a problem with this woman reaching for Him. It doesn't seem to bother Him in the least. In fact, if we can continue reading our story, in Matthew 9:22, the Scriptures say that Jesus turned and saw her, and He spoke three words to her, words that were simple but would have been profound in her first-century Jewish world.

Read Matthew 9:22 and write down those words below.

Next week, when we come together, we are going to learn what a highly unusual statement that was for a rabbi to say to a woman in public two thousand years ago in Jesus's world. I love that He doesn't have a problem in the world with her reaching for Him. He turns and He sees her, and He says, "Take heart, daughter." These three words—this is going to be our theme for our entire feast. Three words. Words printed in red in your Bible, spoken to a woman with a twelve-year issue of blood, in public, grabbing a rabbi, the Sun of Righteousness, the Son of God, Jesus, by His wing.

And if He did it for her, He can do it for you.

Do you believe that last statement? Share your reasons below.

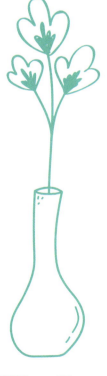

You need to know that Jesus can handle you—your doubts, your failures, your hurts, your longings, your pain. In every possible way, throughout any point in your journey, you have access to Him. He is there for you. And I believe healing is still found in His wing.

{ PERSONAL STUDY }

Before You Start: Grab your highlighters or colored pens! We want you to engage as you read, so choose your colors to mark meaningful quotes and insights.

- ☐ Use this color to <u>underline</u> something new you've learned.
- ☐ Use this color to (circle) something you don't want to forget.
- ☐ Use this color to *star* something you need to live out.

Look

TALLIT

The *tallit* (pl. *tallitot*) is a prayer shawl. It has been used (and still is today) in a variety of ways, depending on a person's tradition and orthodoxy. The *tallit* is often worn in prayer and worship.[1] In Numbers 15:37-40 and Deuteronomy 22:12, the Torah instructed the Israelites to put tassels (*tzitzit*) on the corners of their garments.[2]

> **The LORD said to Moses, "Speak to the Israelites and say to them: 'Throughout the generations to come you are to make tassels on the corners of your garments, with a blue cord on each tassel. You will have these tassels to look at and so you will remember all the commands of the LORD, that you may obey them and not prostitute yourselves by chasing after the lusts of your own hearts and eyes. Then you will remember to obey all my commands and will be consecrated to your God.'"**
> **NUMBERS 15:37-40**

> **Make tassels on the four corners of the cloak you wear.**
> **DEUTERONOMY 22:12**

Each *tzitzit* (tassel) contains several little knots—for a combined total of 613 knots on a *tallit*, each representing one of the commandments in the Torah.[3] Every time the Israelites saw the knots on the tassels, they were to remember the commandments. The Hebrew word used for the corner of the *tallit*, kanafayim (corners), can also mean "wings."[4] Likely, the tassels were permanently fixed on the corners, or wings, of the outer hem of the garment.

The Torah also instructed the Israelites to run a blue or violet cord through the tassels on their *tallitot*. Both rabbinic sources and archaeological data tell us the blue dye used to color these tassels was made from a gland of the Murex snail (originating from the Mediterranean). Each snail produced a very small amount of dye, making it very expensive.[5] Neighboring cultures used the colors blue and violet as symbols and signs for royalty. For the Israelites, this blue or violet cord may have been a sign or a symbol of the royal status of the entire community.

This idea of the royalty of the nation of Israel was tied to God's covenant relationship with them. The Israelites were not royal because of any worldly qualifications, but they were a royal community because they were God's people (see Deut. 7:6-7). God set them apart with His love, and His love lifted them up.

God's choice to remind His people of their royal lineage in Him is especially impactful when you consider the fabric of Israelite culture and their national identity at the time God gave them this instruction. When God told them to run regal cords through their tassels, the

Torah

Just as Christians have divided the Old Testament into categories (i.e., Law, History, Poetry, Major Prophets, Minor Prophets), the Jews have divided their sacred text. *Torah* is a section of Jewish Scripture that includes instruction and the Law. For the Jews, nothing is more important than Torah. It's the first place they go when deriving authority from Scripture. The books of Torah include Genesis, Exodus, Leviticus, Numbers, and Deuteronomy—what scholars today call the *Pentateuch* (literally "five books"). Though traditionally translated as "law," the word *Torah* implies instruction more than law. According to Torah, the commandments offer freedom more than oppression. They serve as parameters that allow a person to function well in their family, tribe, and nation.[6]

Each knot represents one of God's commandments—instructions to live in shalom—as a way of keeping His way of life in front of His people.

GOD NOT ONLY FREED THE ISRAELITES FROM SLAVERY, BUT HE ALSO IMMEDIATELY REMINDED THEM THAT HE MADE THEM REGAL AND ROYAL.

people were still working to shed the national identity they had borne for so many years as Egyptian slaves. God not only freed them from that slavery, but He also immediately reminded them that He had made them regal and royal. It was as if God was saying, "I know what Egypt said you were and how you were mistreated there. But I say you are a royal priesthood, a holy nation set apart by My love. Live in the identity I have given to you, forgetting any other label the world has tried to place on you."

READ MATTHEW 9:20-22.

In Matthew 9 we see a woman with an ongoing "issue of blood" that had lasted twelve years. This condition would have rendered her unclean according to Jewish law, which would have had some significant effects on her day-to-day life. She would not have been able to attend temple or synagogue, because her condition would have deemed her as unclean. This would have left her cut off from the religious community and teaching. God's people and God's house, places where we often find refuge and solace today—especially in times of suffering—would not have been a refuge for her. In fact, the religious community would have effectively turned its back on her and avoided association with her.

Despite the communal nature of the Middle Eastern culture, she would have been considered on the "outside" of the social world—essentially, she would have been socially dead. This woman would have been shunned from society to the point that even her family members would not have been allowed to touch her or comfort her physically, because it would have made them ceremonially unclean and excluded from the community until they could be ritually cleansed.[7] It's hard for us to fathom how alone she must have felt.

Take a moment to imagine what this woman's world and life must have been like. What do you think she would have most desired? What do you think might have caused her the greatest pain?

This woman, the one who had been dealing with years of pain—physical, emotional, and spiritual—reached for the "edge" of Jesus's cloak (v. 20). The Greek word for "edge" used in this passage is *kraspedon*.[8] This same word appears in the Septuagint (the Greek translation of the Old Testament) in reference to the tassels that all Jews fixed on the "edges" or "corners/wings" of their outer garments. The Hebrew word for "edge" is *kanafayim*.

The woman with the issue of blood reached for Jesus's healing *kanafayim/kraspedon*—corner, edge, wing—of His *tallit*. This scene in Matthew 9 seems to be a literal fulfillment of Malachi 4:2.

READ MALACHI 4:2.

Consider what it must have taken for this woman to reach out to Jesus—a woman who had been isolated from the community of God's people and access to spiritual teaching. I believe this woman acted out of significant faith. I think that in reaching out to grab the wing of Jesus's *tallit*, she was taking God at His Word in Malachi 4:2 and was asserting her belief in Jesus as the Son of God. In spite of all she had been through, in spite of the way the religious community had probably shunned her, she exerted faith in Jesus. She placed her hope in God's promises, in God's character.

And don't miss this: in that moment, Jesus rewarded her faith, healed her, *and* brought her back to life within her Jewish community. He provided physical and spiritual healing. By reaching out to her, He helped usher her back into society and stuck up for her in the eyes of the world. In her cultural context, the idea of someone unclean touching a holy rabbi like Jesus would have been scandalous and risky. According to the tradition of the day, Jesus would have had every right to react harshly toward her and dismiss her—maybe even kill her.[9]

Pay close attention to Jesus's reaction here. He doesn't condemn. He doesn't dismiss. Instead, the Bible says Jesus turns to her, He sees her, and He says, "Take heart, daughter . . . your faith has healed you" (Matt. 9:22). What a gospel-gorgeous truth. Praise the Living God.

> In what area of your life do you need to hear God say, "Take heart, daughter"? Use a journal or the blank pages in the back of this book to describe it. Write down how the story from Matthew 9 encourages you in that circumstance.

Learn

CARRYING THE WILDERNESS WITH YOU

READ EXODUS 3:1-10.

*Look at this Bible passage through the **Western lens**, asking the question, "How did it happen?" Write down what you notice in this story.*

To review the Western and Middle Eastern Lenses, flip back to page 13.

*Look at this Bible passage through the **Middle Eastern lens**, asking he question, "Why would God do that?" Write down what you notice in this story.*

This story happened in the desert, in the wilderness. Moses was tending his father-in-law's flock on "the far side of the wilderness" (v. 1). We often think of a desert or wilderness as something we want to get *out* of. But the Jewish people view the desert as the place where the Lord often meets His people and speaks to them.

For example, in Exodus 3, the Lord met Moses in the desert and spoke to him. The Lord gave His Torah to His people at Mount Sinai in the desert (see Ex. 20). He met Elijah in the desert and spoke to him in "a still small voice" (1 Kings 19:12, KJV). The Spirit led Jesus into the desert after His baptism, where we see angels attending to Him after His forty-day fast, His encounter with the devil, and His temptations (see Matt. 4:1-11).

In the desert—the wilderness—God meets you and teaches you unique lessons that these dry and barren places frame in ways no other place would. In the Middle Eastern culture, the wilderness is seen almost as a sacred place, a place of intimacy, where God speaks a "word" (*davar*) to you. [10]

This story of Moses in the desert is about the Living God who "[saw] the misery of [His] people in Egypt" (Ex. 3:7a). He "heard them crying out because of their slave drivers" (v. 7b). He was "concerned about their suffering" (v. 7b). He responded to what He saw and heard by coming down to rescue them.

In the Bible, when we read that the Lord "sees" or "hears" something, those words signal to us that He is going to *act*. It's not as if God has missed something—as if He were a human who could turn away and miss a glimpse or whisper of something that has happened. God is omnipresent; He sees and hears everything that happens to us. God is responsive, alive, awake—ever-ready to come to the rescue, to attend to His children in guidance and love.

This story isn't so much about a burning bush but about the Living God who refuses to look away. He chooses to see, to hear, to let it matter—to let it all matter. And it's about the Living God who isn't afraid to come down, get in the middle of the ruins of this world, and put His hands all over them to restore us. We run *from* drama. The Lord runs *into* it to bring rescue, restoration, and renewal.

When we are in a desert or wilderness season of life, we often ask, "How long do I have to be in this wilderness or desert?" Or we ask, "How do I get out of this difficult wilderness season?" But in the Middle East, they ask the questions, "How do I carry the wilderness with me?" "How do I remember the word the Lord taught me in the wilderness?"

THE LIVING GOD ISN'T AFRAID TO COME DOWN, GET IN THE MIDDLE OF THE RUINS OF THIS WORLD, AND PUT HIS HANDS ALL OVER THEM TO RESTORE US.

Are you more likely to fear wilderness/desert seasons, trying to get out of them as quickly as possible, or do you usually see them as a time of growth and intimacy with God, despite the difficulty? Explain.

What would need to change in your heart for you to trust God more fully in wilderness seasons?

Who do you know who's going through a wilderness season right now?

How can you encourage that person to listen for God in the desert?

LIVING FORWARD

Therefore I am now going to allure her;
I will lead her into the wilderness
and speak tenderly to her.
There I will give her back her vineyards,
and will make the Valley of Achor a door of hope.
There she will respond as in the days of her youth,
as in the day she came up out of Egypt.
"In that day," declares the LORD,
"you will call me 'my husband';
you will no longer call me 'my master.'
I will betroth you to me forever;
I will betroth you in righteousness and justice,
in love and compassion.
I will betroth you in faithfulness,
and you will acknowledge the LORD."
HOSEA 2:14-16,19-20

You may be familiar with the message of the book of Hosea. The prophet Hosea (under the inspiration of the Holy Spirit) compared God's relationship with His people to a marriage relationship—a marriage in which Israel was repeatedly unfaithful to God.

In the Hosea 2 passage above, we find an almost shocking illustration of God's covenant faithfulness to His children. The Living God marries His people in the wilderness, the desert, despite their unfaithfulness to the covenant He made with them. This passage pictures God's extraordinary, sacrificial love.

Israel would go on to do its worst while God did His best. Israel would chase after the gods of the nations. In other words, the bride in this illustration, Israel, would not live up to its marriage vows. Just as Gomer was unfaithful in her marriage to Hosea (see 3:1), Israel was unfaithful to God. But God's love runs

longer than our sin, and His atonement covers the whole of our sin. God and God alone would keep the marriage covenant. The Lord married Israel knowing its people would not be able to keep every law, every commandment, or every vow. He did it because He knew He could and would. He knew that the Lamb of God would come one day to take away every sin.

The Lord drew Israel into the desert and spoke to the people there—the place that seemed to only represent barrenness became one of restoration and redemption, of covenant pledge, of love everlasting. To me, Hosea 2 is one of the most beautiful passages in the whole Bible. It is so intimate, so intentional—the covenant love and promise of the Lord given to His people *in* the desert.

The Lord often speaks to His people in a special way in wilderness seasons. We want to carry these lessons and these times of intimate fellowship from the wilderness with us as we live and walk forward.

> When was the last time you were in a desert or wilderness season? Describe the situation below.

> What did you learn during that time?

How did you see God respond on your behalf in that wilderness season?

How can the things learned in that wilderness season travel forward with you and strengthen you as you live your life?

How can you keep the lessons of the wilderness with you instead of dismissing them or trying to forget them?

Session Three

JESUS AND WOMAN IN THE FIRST-CENTURY WORLD

{ THE FEAST }

As we pull up our chairs for Session Three of this biblical feast, we are again posturing ourselves to receive—to be fed the Word of God by the Lord Himself. In some ancient way, He has set this table for us, and He is the One who has drawn us to it. He wants to meet us *in* this feast, at the table He is preparing for us. Remember, we want to stare at the Lord and glance at our lives.

BEGIN

As we begin our feast, take a few moments to answer the following questions before you watch the video teaching.

> What have you been thinking about since last week's feast?

> Who did you live like a river toward last week by sharing what you learned at the feast?

> How did that conversation go? How did your time together challenge you or confirm what you've been learning?

Use the following space or the blank pages at the back of this book during our feast teaching time to add your own notes as you watch.

THE TEACHING SESSION BUNDLE IS AVAILABLE FOR PURCHASE AT LIFEWAY.COM/JESUSANDWOMEN

WESTERN LENS	MIDDLE EASTERN LENS
Form	Function
How? *How did it happen?*	Why? *Why would God do that?*
Understand → Believe	Believe → Understand
Law, Rule, Principle	Story, Narrative
What does it teach me about *me*?	What does it teach me about *God*?
Dig deep, get down in it . . . *(Analysis—pick it apart)*	Read through it . . . *(Synthesis—bring it together)*
Study to acquire *knowledge*	Posture to be *fed*

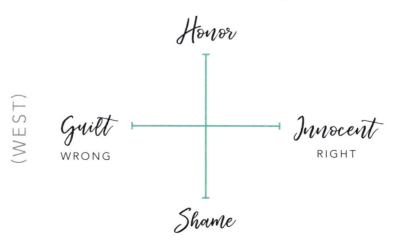

(MIDDLE EAST)

Honor

(WEST)

Guilt
WRONG

Innocent
RIGHT

Shame

{ YESHIVA }

Each week we're going to take some time to *yeshiva*—to emulate the Middle Eastern communal way of discussing spiritual concepts and growing together in grace as a biblical community.

What did you just *hear* or *see* in our feast together that you want to remember?

In our feast this week, we looked at two things that were present in every interaction Jesus had with a woman in the New Testament Gospels. In each story, Jesus brought two things into the woman's life: *mishpat* and *tzedakah*.

Do you remember what each of these words mean? Describe them in your own words.

- *Mishpat:*

- *Tzedakah:*

READ PSALM 89:14.

What are the foundations of God's throne?

Translated most often as "justice," the Hebrew word mishpat serves a special function in the economy of God. Since God advocates for the poor and the oppressed, especially widows and orphans, He expects His followers to do the same. At its core, *mishpat* isn't so much a question of innocence and guilt as much as it is a matter of honor and shame. To bring justice to the world, God exalts the humble by raising them up to honor and covering their shame.

Tied closely to the word *tzedakah*, or "righteousness," *mishpat* deals with punishment for wrongdoing, but it's also concerned about equal rights for all—rich and poor, female and male, foreigner and native-born.[1]

How does God offer you *mishpat* (justice) in your life?

Oftentimes, when we think of righteousness, or **tzedakah**, we think of cleanness. I was sinful, and I have been made righteous through the blood of Jesus Christ. I was unclean; I have been made clean.

While *tzedakah* does mean "righteousness," it also means so much more. *Tzedakah* can be described as "generosity towards others," or even easily translated as "mercy." In the first-century world, giving to the poor was seen as an act of righteousness. (See Matt. 6:1-4.) By not sharing generously, one violates the very justice, will, and command of God. Therefore, when you give, it is an act of righteousness. *Tzedakah* is not optional in God's economy.[2]

How has God brought *tzedakah* (righteousness) into your life?

In the Middle East, to have a *good eye* means you are generous.[2] Who is the most generous person you know? Why do you consider them to be generous? Do you have a *good eye*?

We also learned in our feast this week that woman had a good beginning, a good genesis. God created woman with dignity and honor, and the culture of early civilization recognized the *imago dei* in her. From the very beginning of the story, God had a very good plan, a very good purpose, and a very good perspective on the feminine and for women.

Is this hard for you to believe? Why or why not?

Through our sketch of history, we saw how the rise of Alexander the Great caused a cultural shift where woman had lost her honorable standing in society's eyes. When Jesus came onto the scene, it was into that world that He would come. He would come to bring woman out of her shame and restore her honor.

Look at the chart on page 39. What comes to mind when you see this chart through the Middle Eastern lens? How does this give you a better picture of who Jesus is?

If you want to know who Jesus is when it comes to you as a young woman, He's the one who meets you in your deepest place of shame, looks at you right in the middle of your story, and lifts you up. He is restoring your honor and inviting you to live forward from that place. That is who He is. That is what He's like.

Do you have a story about a time when God generously lifted you up? If so, write it below and share it with your group.

For the next five weeks, we're getting ready to eat stories throughout the Gospels that involve Jesus interacting with women. In each story, you're going to learn to see the *mishpat* and *tzedakah*— the justice and righteousness—and how God desires to generously lift you up from shame and restore your honor.

ABUNDANT LIFE

"Scripture is like a river . . . broad and deep; shallow enough here for the lamb to go wading but deep enough there for the elephant to swim." [3]
—Gregory The Great

The Bible is living and active, and so are we. When we sit down with our Bibles, it is life with life—the life that God has placed in us through His Holy Spirit interacting with the living Word of God. And when the living Word of God collides with the life of God inside of us it generates more life. This is what the Jews call *l'chaim*—a phrase that literally means "to life!" [4]

A flourishing. An abundance.

Time spent with God refines and fine-tunes us in order to help us understand how God created life to be. He brings the best of life to us. The world and its circumstances take up so much of our time and emotional energy, but the Bible gives us a glimpse into of what is true about God, about us, and about the world around us. We take it in; we let it do its work.

Re-read the quote from Gregory the Great above. When it comes to your relationship with the Bible, do you feel more like a lamb or an elephant? Why?

Do you believe that God's Word and ways bring you abundant life? Do you believe this intellectually and in the way you live? Explain.

{ PERSONAL STUDY }

Before You Start: Grab your highlighters or colored pens! We want you to engage as you read, so choose your colors to mark meaningful quotes and insights.

- ☐ Use this color to <u>underline</u> something new you've learned.
- ☐ Use this color to ⊙circle something you don't want to forget.
- ☐ Use this color to *star* something you need to live out.

Look

HULDAH

We have one more addition to the list of godly Israelite women in the Old Testament that we discussed in our feast this week—Huldah, a prophetess during the reign of King Josiah. Second Kings 22–23 and 2 Chronicles 34 tell her story.

READ 2 KINGS 22–23.

From this story, we come to understand that the *Torah*, the Law that told God's people how to please Him and that governed the nation of Israel, had been lost for some time. When the long-lost Torah was discovered in the temple by Hilkiah, the high priest, it was brought to King Josiah. Shaphan, the secretary, read it aloud to Josiah. After hearing it, Josiah tore his

Beit

Beit is the Hebrew word for "house." In Jesus's first-century world, hospitality and communal living were central to the culture. So it should come as no surprise that the ideas of house and affiliation were also very important. You were not so much known for your job or your work, but for your people and the house you were part of. Solomon built the Lord a temple—or a *beit* (house). The temple in Jerusalem was the Lord's house. He lived in Jerusalem with and among His people.[5]

robes, a sign of grief and mourning in the Hebrew culture (see 2 Kings 22:11). Josiah realized how deeply Israel had strayed from the way of the Lord as prescribed in the Law. He saw firsthand how far Israel had fallen in terms of obedience to the Lord God. King Josiah ruled a nation in need of deep repentance, change, reform, and revival.

What should he do? With the nation on the line, to which of God's prophets would Josiah reach out for counsel? King Josiah had several prophets at his disposal—Jeremiah, Zephaniah, Nahum, Habakkuk, and Huldah. I imagine the names of the first four prophets just mentioned are familiar to you; each of these men penned books, through the inspiration of the Holy Spirit, that are now part of Israel's collection of prophets (our Old Testament) and are named after them.

It might seem like the logical choice to consult one of those men—it's clear God used them mightily in their time. But although he had this wealth of wise prophets to choose from, King Josiah consulted Huldah. She prophesied that disaster would fall upon Jerusalem and the kingdom of Judah. She also prophesied that Josiah would not see this calamity in his lifetime, because his heart had been responsive and humble before the Lord. Both of these prophecies came to pass.

Because of Huldah's role in Josiah's reforms, she became a well-known figure in Israel's history. Together with Josiah, Huldah was credited with helping turn the nation of Israel back to God and consequently sparing a generation of God's people from His wrath and judgment. Years later, when Herod's temple was built in Jerusalem (expanding Zerubbabel's temple), the gates where pilgrims and worshipers entered and exited the temple were named the Huldah Gates. Huldah's name was known by all who came to Jerusalem to worship the Living God at His *beit* (house).

HULDAH WAS CREDITED WITH HELPING TURN THE NATION OF ISRAEL BACK TO GOD AND CONSEQUENTLY SPARING A GENERATION OF GOD'S PEOPLE.

The two Huldah Gates on the south were used both for entrance and exit.[6]
MISHNAH MIDDOT 1:3

Mishnah

When God gave His Torah to Moses at Mount Sinai, Jews believe He also gave a second set of laws called Mishnah or "that which is repeated." [7] According to this line of thinking, the written Torah (or *Mikra*) was far greater in importance, but the oral Torah (or *Mishnah*) expanded and explained the meaning of the written Torah.

By the beginning of the third century AD, a man known as Yehudah ha-Nasi, or in English, Judah the Prince, led a project to record the traditions that had been handed down to that point. [8]

This written document offers a small window into Judaism from 300 BC to approximately AD 200. [9] It is divided into six main sections, with those subdivided into seven to twelve subsections, starting with the longest and ending with the shortest. [10]

It is incredible to think that the very gates by which people entered the temple of God were named after a woman. What an honor!

When I take teams to Israel, we sit in front of the Huldah Gates on the Southern Rabbinic Teaching Steps that lead up to the southern wall of the Temple Mount for one of our biblical classes. For hundreds of years, pilgrims would come to Jerusalem in observance of the three "foot festivals" given in Deuteronomy 16—Passover, Pentecost (the Feast of Weeks), and the Feast of Tabernacles. (In Middle Eastern culture, many things are named or labeled literally. These were called "foot festivals" because the people traveled by foot three times a year to attend them.)

As the worshipers ascended the Southern Steps to enter the temple through the Huldah Gates, they may have sung the psalms of ascent (see Pss. 120–134), psalms of praise written for the pilgrimage to the temple. [11] These psalms are rhythmic and melodic. Worshipers during that time didn't simply read the psalms the way we do— they sang them. Imagine traveling to Jerusalem from far away. You've finally reached the city after a long journey, and as you walk up the steps to enter God's house (temple), you sing the following:

I lift up my eyes to the mountains—
where does my help come from?
My help comes from the LORD
the Maker of heaven and earth.
He will not let your foot slip—
he who watches over you will not slumber;
indeed, he who watches over Israel
will neither slumber nor sleep.
The LORD watches over you—
the LORD is your shade at your right hand;
the sun will not harm you by day,
nor the moon by night.
The LORD will keep you from all harm—

he will watch over your life;
*the L*ORD *will watch over your coming and going*
both now and forevermore.

PSALM 121

It would have been such a celebratory moment, seeing the house of God—where your help comes from—with the long pilgrimage over, ready to finally be in the presence of the one true God. I imagine worshipers experienced levity, laughter, and joy upon arriving at the Lord's house to worship Him with their Israelite brothers and sisters.

MANNA

READ EXODUS 16:1-5,13-17,31-36.

Look at this Bible passage through the **Western lens**, *the framework of understanding first then allowing that understanding to fuel belief. Write down what you notice in this story.*

Look at this Bible passage through the **Middle Eastern lens**, *the framework of believing first then allowing that belief to fuel understanding. Write down what you notice in this story.*

In this beautiful story, we see a moment when the Israelites believed God and understanding followed.

The book of Exodus tells the story of the Hebrews' liberation from Egyptian tyranny and slavery. After around 430 years of slavery and forced labor in Egypt, the Lord miraculously delivered them out of Egypt, through the Red Sea. [12] Those years of slavery changed them. When they crossed the Red Sea to their freedom, they were an exhausted, disoriented, and confused people. With Egypt behind them and the desert in front of them, the Israelites walked into an unknown future with God.

HE IS TRUSTWORTHY. YOU CAN AFFORD TO BELIEVE HIM, TO TAKE HIM AT HIS WORD, AND *THEN* WALK INTO UNDERSTANDING.

The people of God, freshly liberated from slavery, had no idea how to live free after something like 430 years of bondage. They were in the desert, and they were hungry. One morning they woke up, walked out of their tents, looked down on the ground, and saw something—something they had never seen before.

> **When the Israelites saw it, they said to each other, "What is it?" For they did not know what it was.**
> EXODUS 16:15

In Exodus 16 we read the account of when the Lord began providing *manna* for His people. The Bible calls it "bread from heaven" (Ex. 16:4). Manna was also described as "white like coriander seed and [tasting] like wafers made with honey" (v. 31).

The Hebrew word for manna is manhue (also sometimes transliterated ha-man)— and the sense of the word comes in the form of a question. *Manhue* means, "What is it?" [13] The Israelites were hungry; they ate the manna without knowing what it was. They ate a mystery because they knew it came from the hand of God. They trusted the source and bit down on the unknown—literally.

They ate the "What is it?" and found out exactly what it was—God's faithful provision for them in the desert for what, unbeknownst to them, would be forty years. He provided manna every day except for the Sabbath; on the day before the Sabbath, He provided the Israelites with two days worth of food. The Lord never failed them. He never went on vacation and forgot about them. Most important of all, He never ran out. God's people learned that His provision is inexhaustible; He continues to give and give. He is trustworthy. You can afford to believe Him, to take Him at His word, and *then* walk into understanding.

Is there a difficult situation, circumstance, or relationship in your life right now, one it's hard to believe God could ever change? Describe it below.

Can you recount, remember, or retell the story of a time in your life when God met you in a struggle or provided for you? Describe it below.

How can that past story of struggle and remembering God's provision encourage you in the difficult situation you're currently facing?

The Israelites ate manna forty years, until they came to a land that was settled; they ate manna until they reached the border of Canaan.
EXODUS 16:35

On the evening of the fourteenth day of the month, while camped at Gilgal on the plains of Jericho, the Israelites celebrated the Passover. The day after the Passover, that very day, they ate some of the produce of the land: unleavened bread and roasted grain. The manna stopped the day after they ate this food from the land; there was no longer any manna for the Israelites, but that year they ate of the produce of Canaan.
JOSHUA 5:10-12

God's provision for His children was so precise that He stopped sending manna the day after the Israelites ate the fruit of the land of Canaan. His promised provision carried them to the promised land. Like the Israelites, we are living on the Lord's promises to us, and He will not let us down.

But He doesn't promise to tell us everything that's going on ahead of time. He doesn't promise we'll see a blueprint before we start building. The reward is often on the other side of obedience. The Levites stepped into the Jordan River with the ark of the covenant and *then* the waters split (see Josh. 3). We don't always get all the facts before we need to make a decision. But we can always decide to trust God's character. We can always decide to believe in God's goodness and steadfast love.

Eating a mystery requires faith in the God who is providing the mystery. If we wait until we understand it all, we will never move, never set out, never know what could have been. Waiting until we understand the situation can render us paralyzed of heart—too afraid to lean into the new and next things because they are unknown.

We look into the mystery and say, "What is it?" When you know it's the Lord leading, prompting, speaking, moving—eat the mystery. Lean into it and see where it takes you. Lean into the mystery and watch the Living God provide.

In what situation, circumstance, or relationship in your life right now do you think God might be asking you to believe Him and trust Him before you fully understand? Describe it below.

What, if anything, is keeping you from trusting God with this situation, circumstance, or relationship? Explain.

Do you believe the reward is often on the other side of obedience? Why or why not?

Live

EATING A MYSTERY

The Israelites ate manna in the desert for forty years until they entered Canaan. *Manhue* is a question—"What is it?" In the desert, the Israelites ate a mystery, something they did not know or understand, because they knew it came from the Lord. Sometimes in His provision for us, the Lord asks us to trust Him and move forward without having all the answers, to trust He will sustain us even in the things that feel like a mystery to us. We tend to be a people who want certainty, clarity, surety, and full understanding *before* we move, but God doesn't promise to provide those answers every time.

Can you think of a time when you "ate the mystery" because you knew it was the Lord leading you, prompting you, or guiding you into something unknown?

When was the last time you said "yes" to something without having all the facts first?

How did it turn out? Are you still in the midst of it?

Call, text, or email a friend this week and ask her to share a story of a time when she "ate a mystery," too. Sharing our stories of God's provision brings Him glory, and it serves to fuel our future faith.

Session Four

JESUS
AND THE
WOMAN AT
THE WELL

{ THE FEAST }

We are getting ready to pull up our chairs for Session Four of this biblical feast. More than reading the Word of God, we seek to eat it. We want to take it in and let it do its work. We approach the Word as daughters—we lean back, look up, open wide our mouths, and trust God will feed us. We posture ourselves to receive.

BEGIN

As we begin our feast, take a few moments to answer the following questions before you watch the video teaching.

What have you been thinking about since last week's feast?

Who did you live like a river toward last week by sharing what you learned at the feast?

How did that conversation go? How did your time together challenge you or confirm what you've been learning?

Use the following space or the blank pages at the back of this book during our feast teaching time to add your own notes as you watch.

THE TEACHING SESSION BUNDLE IS AVAILABLE FOR PURCHASE AT LIFEWAY.COM/JESUSANDWOMEN

WESTERN LENS	MIDDLE EASTERN LENS
Form	Function
How? *How did it happen?*	Why? *Why would God do that?*
Understand → Believe	Believe → Understand
Law, Rule, Principle	Story, Narrative
What does it teach me about *me*?	What does it teach me about *God*?
Dig deep, get down in it . . . (Analysis—*pick it apart*)	Read through it . . . (Synthesis—*bring it together*)
Study to acquire *knowledge*	Posture to be *fed*

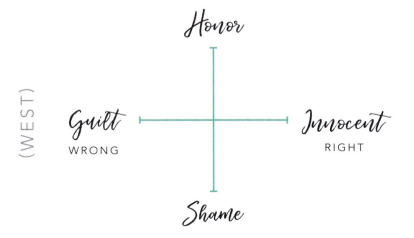

(MIDDLE EAST)

Honor

(WEST)

Guilt
WRONG

Innocent
RIGHT

Shame

{ YESHIVA }

Each week we're going to take some time to *yeshiva*—to emulate the Middle Eastern communal way of discussing spiritual concepts and growing together in grace as a biblical community.

> What did you just *hear* or *see* in our feast together that you want to remember?

In our time together, we took a glimpse at the story found in John 4. You learned about the seven-hundred-year-old history of tension and disagreement between the Jews and Samaritans. But in John 4:4, we read that Jesus "had to go through Samaria." Jesus is doing something unusual here; history tells us many Galilean Jews avoided Samaria altogether on their way to Jerusalem, going out of their way to go around the region where Samaritans lived even if it would take longer. [1]

Why might Jesus have "had" to go through Samaria? I think Jesus *chose* to go through Samaria because He wanted to bring restoration to that deep and ancient schism between the Jews and Samaritans. And we see in John 4 that this unusual route became an opportunity for Jesus to bring *mishpat* and *tzedakah* to a Samaritan woman.

> **READ JOHN 4:1-30.**

> According to verse 7, at what time did the woman go to the well to draw water?

The women in the village would have gone to the well very early in the morning. But here this woman finds herself at a well in the middle of the day, alone. Something automatically tells us this is not okay, because she has no help.

She is missing a *haver.*

A *haver* is a friend—somebody who helps you carry your water. This isn't just someone you just go to a football game with or follow on social media. Your true *haver* helps you carry your water—they shoulder the weight of life in your story.

Who is your *haver*?

Who are you a *haver* to? Who might need you to be their *haver*?

This woman was alone, but Jesus sat with her in her pain. Then He started generously lifting her up. Here's how:

- Her named her shame, not her sin.
- He reached out to her and spoke first—He bridged the gap.
- He asked if He could drink after her, treating her as clean, not unclean.
- He respected her by talking theology of worship with her. She was the first person He told that He was the Messiah.

Which of these points of lifting up do you need the most right now? Explain why.

haver
(PL. HAVERIM)

A Hebrew word literally meaning "friend" or "companion." In the first-century world, a *haver* was a study partner and fellow disciple—someone you could ask hard questions of and someone whom you could expect to ask you hard questions in return.

Haverim pushed each other, sometimes to the brink, in order to get to the truth. If you called someone your *haver* in the first-century world, it also implied that you followed the Torah in a similar fashion. You might even follow the same rabbi.

You might spend the majority of your days with these *haverim* discussing the most important issues in your life and the lives of those around you.[2]

If Jesus did it for her, do you believe Jesus can do it for you? Take a moment to get alone in prayer to ask Him to lift you where you need it most.

DEVOURING GOD'S WORD

But their delight is in the law of the LORD, and on his law they meditate day and night.
PSALM 1:2 (NRSV)

When you think of meditating on a passage of Scripture, what imagery or actions come to mind?

I'm not sure what you wrote in your answer above. But when I think of "meditating" in our cultural context today, I usually think of something quiet that includes pondering an idea or spiritual truth, an activity I might do alone. But that's not what the original audience of the Bible would have had in mind when they read Psalm 1:2. This is a great example of how we tend to interpret biblical words and concepts using meanings and imagery that are common to us today.

Men *"hagah-ing"* a passage of Scripture.

This word "meditate" in the original Hebrew language is *hagah*. [3] It means to eat or devour something, like a lion eats its prey. [4] The sense of the word is fierce and active.

Jesus was born into a culture with an oral communication tradition. Rabbis memorized the Old Testament texts and taught the Scriptures from memory. Spiritual growth was often in the context of community. Spiritual leaders taught the Scriptures orally. Those in spiritual community with one another would then dialogue about what a Bible passage meant, in a sense wrestling with God's Word as a community of faith. Their community of faith and communal contending with God's Word fed their personal faith and devotion. In this line of thinking, followers of God grapple with His Word to understand who He is and to walk His path of life, to live in a way that pleases God, obeying Him and flourishing under His care. "*Hagah*-ing" a passage led to obedience, walking the path of life with God.

In some ways, our Western understanding of meditating on God's Word is similar to the context of the original Hebrew. When we *hagah* a passage, we take it in, and it becomes a part of who we are. It fuels our devotion to God. In the first century, Jews would describe a spiritual truth that they meditated on as "becoming a part of their fabric"—in other words, becoming a part of who they were. When we turn a spiritual truth over and over in our hearts and minds, it becomes a part of who we are; it becomes "a part of our fabric." And with those new truths inside of us, we have the ability to know God more fully and walk the path of life with Him.

We can *hagah*—meditate on—a passage alone, but eating is much better together. We want to devour the Word of God like a lion eating its prey.

Have you ever thought of reading God's Word like this? What usually comes to mind when you think about Scripture?

What would it look like for you to hagah with this group or with other friends at church?

Before You Start: Grab your highlighters or colored pens! We want you to engage as you read, so choose your colors to mark meaningful quotes and insights.

- ☐ Use this color to <u>underline</u> something new you've learned.
- ☐ Use this color to (circle) something you don't want to forget.
- ☐ Use this color to *star* something you need to live out.

Look

JACOB'S WELL

> *Jacob's well was there, and Jesus, tired as he was from the journey, sat down by the well. It was about noon.*
> JOHN 4:6

When the Lord introduced Himself to Moses in Exodus 3, He said, "I am the God of your father, the God of Abraham, the God of Isaac and the God of Jacob" (Ex. 3:6). Jacob was one of the patriarchal fathers of the Jewish people. Jacob's well was dug in the days of Genesis.

Hundreds and hundreds of years later, Jesus sat with the Samaritan woman at this very well. In Jesus's day, the well was located in a city called Sychar, at the base of *Mount Gerizim*—the mountain the Samaritan woman mentioned, the one where the Samaritans worshiped. [5] The Samaritans had built a temple on the top of Mount Gerizim because they were not permitted to worship at the temple in Jerusalem. [6]

Jacob's well still exists today—some nearly two thousand years after Jesus sat at it with the Samaritan woman. The name of the city where it's located has changed: it's now called Nablus. The well is still located at the base of Mount Gerizim. To this very day, Samaritans still live on Mount Gerizim, and you can see the ruins and remains of the Samaritan temple toward the top of the mountain.

Jacob's well is one of my favorite sites. I love taking teams to Jacob's well when we are in the Holy Land. While we're there, I invite the women to circle around the well and read the entire story of John 4 out loud, one verse at a time.

Jacob's well as it appears today

I love giving women that special moment—reading the story of the woman at the very well where the story took place some two thousand years earlier.

After we read the story in John 4, the women then take turns winding the crank and bringing water up from Jacob's well in a tin pail. The well still produces water—cool and clear.

In a similar way, this story still moves us, speaks to us, and travels through us as we share it with others. The Bible isn't just the best story ever told—it is also the truest. These stories really happened. Jesus really came to earth to set things right. The Bible shows us how God designed the world to work, how He made our hearts, and how life really is.

How does knowing that the Bible is the truest story ever told change the way you read it?

Learn

HILLEL VS. SHAMMAI

READ MATTHEW 19:1-9.

 *Look at this Bible passage through the **Western lens**, identifying the law, rule, or principle at hand. Write down what you notice in this story.*

 *Look at this Bible passage through the **Middle Eastern lens**, identifying it as part of the biblical story or narrative. Write down what you notice in this story.*

One generation before Jesus, there were two main religious houses or schools in Jerusalem. Both schools were very influential throughout Judaism and maintained incredibly influential leaders as their heads.

One school followed *Rabbi Hillel* [7] and the other *Rabbi Shammai*. [8] Hillel's grandson was named Gamaliel. You may recognize his name; he was the rabbi who the apostle Paul studied under (see Acts 22:3).

Hillel was a "spirit of the law" kind of guy. Shammai, on the other hand, was a "letter of the law" kind of guy. Hillel and Shammai often read the same Scripture and came up with different interpretations and methods of application. Hillel was usually wider in his interpretations, meaning he typically gave more grace and leeway in places where the law was more open to interpretation. Shammai was usually much more narrow in his interpretations, meaning he was typically more rigid and conservative when the law proved somewhat ambiguous. [9]

During Hillel and Shammai's day there was a widespread debate over the interpretation of Deuteronomy 24:1. It was one of the hot topics in their generation. [10]

> *"If a man marries a woman who becomes displeasing to him because he finds something indecent about her, and he writes her a certificate of divorce, gives it to her and sends her from his house."*
> DEUTERONOMY 24:1

The debate of the day centered on what the word "indecent" meant in this Deuteronomy text in the Torah. Whatever "indecent" meant, it was grounds for a man to divorce his wife and send her away.

According to Rabbi Hillel, "indecent" could be many things. In Hillel's view, a man could divorce his wife for something as simple as burning the bread, among many other things. [11]

Rabbi Shammai taught a very different interpretation of the word "indecent." For Shammai, the only indecent thing that provided grounds for a man to divorce his wife was adultery. [12]

In Jesus's world, men alone had the power to divorce their wives; a woman could not initiate divorce proceedings against her husband. This cultural practice created a gender inequity in marriage and left women vulnerable to mistreatment and easy abandonment.

> "The right to divorce was exclusively the husband's." [13]
> —J. JEREMIAS

> "In this way the Hillelite view made the unilateral right of divorce entirely dependent on the husband's caprice." [14]
> —J. JEREMIAS

Jesus came on the scene one generation after Hillel and Shammai. In Matthew 19:3, when the Pharisees asked Jesus the question, "Is it lawful for a man to divorce his wife for any and every reason?" they were in effect asking Him whether He sided with Hillel or Shammai on the issue of divorce. Can a man divorce his wife, abandoning her and leaving her liable and vulnerable simply because she burned the bread?

This wasn't only a question of divorce—it was a gender-specific question. For what reason(s) can a *man* divorce his *wife*? Jesus sided with Shammai on this issue of divorce and generously lifted up the women up of His first-century world. In siding with Shammai, Jesus protected women from being so easily divorced and held husbands accountable.

Jesus brought justice and righteousness to women within the marriage relationship—protecting them, establishing them, and rejecting the idea that a man could divorce his wife for any reason. As we'll continue to see, Jesus advocated for women who were overlooked by society. He reached out to them with radical kindness and grace, and in doing so, He changed their lives.

Live

GENEROUSLY LIFTED UP

He told her, "Go, call your husband and come back."
JOHN 4:16

Jesus met the Samaritan woman at Jacob's well at the base of Mount Gerizim. It was an ordinary day that would become extraordinary in her life and story.

In this moment, Jesus named her shame, not her sin. He reached all the way into her story, saw into her soul, and likely named the hardest and most shameful thing she had ever lived through. He entered into her world with compassion and empathy. Jesus seeks to enter into your world with compassion and empathy, too. Ordinary days become extraordinary when you let Jesus in to generously lift you up.

If Jesus met with you at your kitchen table this week and named your shame—your deepest point of shame in your story—what would it be? Use the space below to journal out a real conversation with the Lord.

Spend some time with Him this week, thinking and praying about that part of your story. Let Jesus name your shame and generously lift you up out of it again and anew.

Session Five

JESUS AND THE WOMAN AT HIS FEET

{ THE FEAST }

We are getting ready to pull up our chairs for Session Five of this biblical feast. Remember, more than reading the Word of God, we seek to *eat* it. For many of us, the best meal we can eat is one we don't have to cook. The Scriptures are a meal prepared for us by our high and holy Father. He sets a table, prepares His Word, and meets us there—communing with us as He feeds us the Word of God.

BEGIN

As we begin our feast, take a few moments to answer the following questions before you watch the video teaching.

What have you been thinking about since last week's feast?

Who did you live like a river toward last week by sharing what you learned at the feast?

How did that conversation go? How did your time together challenge you or confirm what you've been learning?

Use the following space or the blank pages at the back of this book during our feast teaching time to add your own notes as you watch.

THE TEACHING SESSION BUNDLE IS AVAILABLE FOR PURCHASE AT LIFEWAY.COM/JESUSANDWOMEN

WESTERN LENS	MIDDLE EASTERN LENS
Form	Function
How? *How did it happen?*	Why? *Why would God do that?*
Understand → Believe	Believe → Understand
Law, Rule, Principle	Story, Narrative
What does it teach me about *me*?	What does it teach me about *God*?
Dig deep, get down in it . . . *(Analysis—pick it apart)*	Read through it . . . *(Synthesis—bring it together)*
Study to acquire *knowledge*	Posture to be *fed*

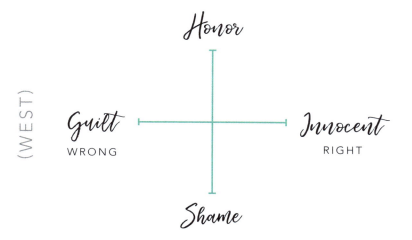

(MIDDLE EAST)

Honor

(WEST)

Guilt
WRONG

Innocent
RIGHT

Shame

YESHIVA

Each week we're going to take some time to *yeshiva*—to emulate the Middle Eastern communal way of discussing spiritual concepts and growing together in grace as a biblical community. Discuss the following questions with your group.

What did you just *hear* or *see* in our feast together that you want to remember?

READ LUKE 7:36-50.

This story happens in the context of table fellowship and in the context of the honorable being allowed to sit at the table, with the marginalized most likely sitting against the wall. Table fellowship and hospitality were some of the highest virtues, or signs of honor, in the culture of Jesus's world. In other words, important stuff happened during meals in Jesus's life and ministry, just as it does today.

Who do you eat with? Who are the people that usually sit with you at your table at home or at school?

Looking at this passage of Scripture, how do you relate to the Pharisee's response to the woman at Jesus's feet?

As a teen girl, what are ways you can practice hospitality? How can you offer a seat to someone who might be marginalized by others?

In verses 41-50, we see Jesus rearrange the room. We see him offer the woman at His feet *mishpat* and *tzedakah*. As the story began, Simon the Pharisee was the honorable host, while the woman was against the wall. But in these verses, we watch Jesus generously lift this woman's position to a place of honor.

How did Jesus respond to the Pharisee?

How did Jesus respond to the woman at His feet?

You have to know: Jesus is not okay with you sitting against a wall. He comes to generously lift you up out of your shame. To restore your honor and to send you away in *shalom*.

How many of you feel like Simon probably never invited Jesus back for dinner? I think that might have been a one and done at Simon's house. But I guarantee you that woman never forgot that night—because when she lost it on a holy Rabbi of Israel, the Messiah, the very Son of God, even to the point of unbinding her hair and wiping His feet with her tears, she would always remember Him as the one who could take that. As the One who contended for her in front of every man who was at that table that night.

When was the last time you really allowed yourself to just pour out your heart to Jesus? To even "lose it" on Him? Is there any disbelief in Him that keeps you from pouring your heart out to Him?

Parashah
(PL. PARASHOT)

Because Torah held the primary place within all of Scripture for the Jews, after the exile, they decided to commit to corporately read all five books aloud throughout the course of a year.[1]

They divided the Torah into fifty-four parashot (or sections), assigning one section of each book to be read at a certain time every year. Thus, every week a new section of Scripture would be studied all week and read aloud in the synagogue for Sabbath.

We find historical evidence for this practice in the Dead Sea Scrolls and the New Testament.[10] In Luke 4, Jesus followed up the Torah reading with a passage from Isaiah. In Acts 15:21, the Jerusalem Council mentioned how the Torah was being read in the synagogues every week.

DAILY BREAD

We brush our teeth every day because it's good for us and keeps us healthy. It's a practice of physical hygiene. Similarly, we practice certain things on a daily basis because they are spiritually good for us—they keep us spiritually healthy. Daily Bible reading is one way we practice spiritual hygiene.

I grew up calling my daily Bible reading a "quiet time." I set this time aside to intentionally be *with* the Lord *in* the Word of God. This daily practice benefited my soul in a way similar to how daily teeth brushing benefited my health. Both are forms of hygiene.

The Jewish people use different language for their weekly Bible reading. They call it the parashah, which means *portion*.[3] They read a certain portion of the Torah (the first five books of the Old Testament Scriptures) every week.[4]

When I think of a *portion*, I often think of eating—of portion control. Last week, we learned about the Hebrew word *hagah*—to devour something like a lion eating its prey. Here again, with this word *parashah*, we see the imagery of *eating* the Scriptures. We take it in. It is sweeter than honey. It becomes part of us, "a part of our fabric," as we live forward from our feasting on the Word of God.

In our Western world, we often think of studying the Scripture, almost reading it academically at times. But the Middle Eastern way is to *sim lev*, to set the Scripture upon the heart, over and over again, so much so that it can't help but seep into your soul—to consume the Scripture so much that it becomes a part of who you are.[5] We want the answer to the question, "Where is the Word of God located?" to be, "Inside of me."

The way we view God's Word is really important because it affects how we know Him and how we come to grow more like Him.

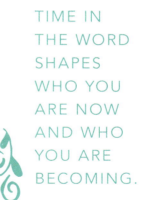

We are striving to create spiritual rhythms in our lives, rather than trying to strong-arm ourselves into spiritual disciplines and checking boxes. In our approach to the Bible—and really any big question we have to answer in our lives—I find it helpful to ask, "Who do you want to be?" God can use the Bible to form you more and more into the image of Christ, if you will *sim lev*—set it on your heart over and over again so that it lives inside of you, so that it becomes a part of who you are. The outworking of growth and joy and hope in our everyday lives comes from inside, from a heart transformed by time with God in His Word. Time in the Word shapes who you are now and who you are becoming.

Take a few moments to consider how you view the Bible and if God may be challenging you to make a change.

How do you view the Bible? As something to learn, or to "eat"?

Do you view your time in the Word as a discipline, a feast, or neither? Do you view it as something you're *supposed* to do? Explain.

Who do you want to be? Is that desire reflected in the way you spend time in God's Word? Explain.

{ PERSONAL STUDY }

Before You Start: Grab your highlighters or colored pens! We want you to engage as you read, so choose your colors to mark meaningful quotes and insights.

- ☐ Use this color to <u>underline</u> something new you've learned.
- ☐ Use this color to (circle) something you don't want to forget.
- ☐ Use this color to *star* something you need to live out.

Look

WALKING IT OUT

You have kept count of my tossings; put my tears in your bottle. Are they not in your record?
PSALM 56:8 (NRSV)

The Psalms are a gift to us. All of Scripture is God's message to us, but in the Psalms, God gives us language to describe every season of life—the joys and pains.

He's giving us permission to bring our most raw emotions and desires to Him, to pour our hearts out to Him. In the Psalms, we're instructed to give the words God has given to us back to Him. They're the language of humanity in every condition and in every state—lament, sadness, grief, anger, fear, regret, worry, and more. The Psalms are a gift, because in them, the Lord equips us with the language we need to bring to Him in prayer when we feel the full range of human emotion. The Lord wants us to share our hearts—our true hearts—with

Him, no matter what we're feeling or thinking. He can handle us. He can handle us telling Him the truth and the whole truth.

> *"How far can we go? How much is permissible? The Psalms suggest that we can go the whole way, that it is all permissible: the praise, yes, but also the grief, the sorrow, the anger . . ."[6]*
> *—Walter Brueggemann*

Jewish people read the Scriptures and seek to live them out, not just know them. They want to *halakh* (walk out) the path of the Lord in accordance with His instructions and laws. When they read something in Scripture, they don't just ponder it or think about it; they act. They try to embody it in the way they live their lives, sometimes literally. They don't just believe it in their hearts; they walk it out in their actions.

What's the difference between a Christian who talks about believing in God versus living this belief out?

Psalm 56:8 speaks of tears being collected in a bottle and of God keeping a record of the tears we've shed in this life. From the days of the Psalms, about one thousand years before the time of Jesus, some Jewish women took this passage to heart and carried in their possessions a *lachrymatory*—a tear jar to use in their worship times. (The word *lachrymatory* is related to the *lacrimal duct*, the spot in the corner of our eyes where our bodies produce tears.)

These Jewish women would collect their tears in tear jars as a tangible way of symbolically collecting their sorrows, sadness, grief, and hurt. They then pour the tear jar out before the Lord in an act of worship, faith, and trust. To pour out one's tear jar is to pour out one's whole heart—the sorrow, sadness, and grief. This practice is a visible way of living out—walking out—Psalm 56:8.

In Psalm 56, God gives value to our tears. He tells us that He sees every hurt and every sorrow. He tells us that He holds our hearts in it all; He walks through it with us. He will bring joy eventually and eternally. In a similar way, the tear jar gives value to tears. They are precious to God. They are worth recognizing, and they are worth keeping. They are worth storing up because of

the One who can handle *all* our tears. The One who can hold *all* of our sadness, grief, sorrow, hurt, and pain can handle it. He can take it.

And He invites you to bring it all to Him and receive His grace and redemption. God wants to generously lift you up and restore what has been broken by this world of pain and sin.

The *lachrymatory* in the photo on the bottom of page 77 was given to me by one of my professors in Israel. It is an actual archaeological artifact dating back to the first or second century AD and was uncovered in Israel.

This tear jar most likely belonged to a Jewish woman in antiquity, maybe even in the time of Jesus's earthly ministry. She might have collected her tears in this very jar. I look at the tear jar often and wonder what her story looked like: what she experienced, her highs and lows. I wonder where she kept her jar and how often she pulled it out to collect her tears before the Lord.

Halakh

In Jesus's first-century world, a Jewish rabbi wasn't interested in teaching philosophy or grand ideas that float around in the sky just for the sake of debate. Philosophy and acquiring knowledge was the ideal of the Greeks, not the Jews. According to the Greeks, education was important because "man is the measure of all things."[7]

For the Jews, the Lord is the Lord of all, and all things should be oriented to Him. A rabbi's teachings were crafted to show you how to *halakh* (walk) the *halakha* (way or path). A rabbi taught you how to walk out your life in the path or way of the Living God. It wasn't about what you thought—it was all about how you lived. It wasn't what you knew—it was about how you walked the path of the Lord.[8]

It's possible the woman in Luke 7 brought two jars to the dinner with Jesus at the home of Simon the Pharisee—two jars for two very different reasons. An alabaster jar of expensive perfume to anoint Jesus, and a tear jar to pour out her sorrows to Him. In this act of worship, it seems she was recognizing Jesus's deity, pouring out her tears to Him—the tears Psalm 56 says God sees and keeps record of.

Jesus could handle both—a mixture of anointing oil and a woman's deepest pain poured out in her tears. We can pour our whole hearts out to Jesus. We can leave it *all* before Him. We can cast it all upon Him. He can take it, and He wants to take it. When we pour out our hearts to Jesus, He begins generously lifting us up in grace and truth. Like the woman in Luke 7, He can lift us up and send us on our way in peace.

How does the practice of the tear jar speak to any misconceptions you've had about God not being able to handle your pain or sorrow?

What does it look like for you to offer your praises to God?

What does it look like for you to present your pains to God?

THE ONE WHO CAN HOLD *ALL* OF OUR SADNESS, GRIEF, SORROW, HURT, AND PAIN CAN HANDLE IT. HE CAN TAKE IT.

Kristi's ancient tear jar

Learn

- -

STARING AT GOD

- -

READ LUKE 7:36-50.

 Look at this Bible passage through the **Western lens,** *asking the question, "What does this teach me about me?" Write down what you notice in this story.*

 Look at this Bible passage through the **Middle Eastern lens,** *asking the question, "What does this teach me about God?" Write down what you notice in this story.*

Now, compare your two lists of observations above.
How are they alike?

How are they different?

This exercise is a great way for us to see some of the differences in what we glean from Bible passages based on the way we approach them and what we look for when we read the Scriptures.

Reading a passage with the question, "What does this teach me about *me*?" in mind often causes us to look down and turn inward, focusing on ourselves. On the other hand, when we read a passage with the question, "What does this teach me about *God*?" in mind we look up and out, staring at Him and glancing at our lives. When we focus on what a passage teaches us about God, we devote more of our time and attention to Him, and the cares of our lives dim in comparison. As we behold Him, we are changed. Staring at God will change us in ways focusing on ourselves never can.

Remember this phrase from the psalm of ascent that we discussed in Session Two:

> **I lift up my eyes to the mountains—where does my help come from?**
> **My help comes from the LORD, the Maker of heaven and earth.**
> PSALM 121:1-2

As daughters of the Living God, let's look to Him for our help, strength, and joy.

Take heart, daughter. He's for us.

Live

TIME WITH JESUS

> *A woman in that town who lived a sinful life learned that Jesus was eating at the Pharisee's house, so she came there with an alabaster jar of perfume. As she stood behind him at his feet weeping, she began to wet his feet with her tears. Then she wiped them with her hair, kissed them and poured perfume on them.*
> LUKE 7:37-38

Jesus met this woman right where she was—relegated to a position of low esteem, to a seat against the wall, not allowed to join the table fellowship at the meal. He accepted her anointing and the tears she may have poured onto His feet. He didn't flinch when she started wiping His feet with her hair, something that would have been culturally unheard of. Jesus could handle her—*all* of her poured out onto Him. He brought a generous justice to her and sent her away in peace.

Jesus can handle you too—*all* of you poured out onto Him.

Take some time this week to get honest with Jesus.

Prioritize time alone with Him, however best suits your personality and season of life.

- Take a walk with Him.
- Make a cup of coffee, climb into your favorite chair, and talk to Him.
- Go for a drive with the Lord and pour your heart out to Him.
- Tell Him what you haven't been telling Him, what you've been holding back.
- Use the following page to journal your heart to the Lord.

Take a moment to pour yourself out onto Him and allow Him to generously lift you up; He will gladly receive you.

You probably don't have a lachrymatory sitting on your bedside table. But I want you to know how important your hurts and sorrows are to the Lord. Draw your own version of a tear jar below, then write in all of the pains and burdens you're carrying. Finish your time by presenting your tears to Him as well as pouring out praise to Him for being good, loving, and holy.

Session Six

JESUS
AND THE
WOMAN WITH
CHUTZPAH

{ THE FEAST }

As we pull up our chairs for Session Six of this biblical feast, we are reminded that more than simply reading the Word of God to learn, we seek to eat it for a transformed heart and life. We pull our chairs up to the biblical table with confidence and faith—confidence in the Lord, our Father, who feeds His children, and faith in His goodness to make sure we are fed to the full. Take a moment to still your heart and posture yourself to receive.

BEGIN

As we begin our feast, take a few moments to answer the following questions before you watch the video teaching.

What have you been thinking about since last week's feast?

Who did you live like a river toward last week by sharing what you learned at the feast?

How did that conversation go? How did your time together challenge you or confirm what you've been learning?

Use the following space or the blank pages at the back of this book during our feast teaching time to add your own notes as you watch.

THE TEACHING SESSION BUNDLE IS AVAILABLE FOR PURCHASE AT LIFEWAY.COM/JESUSANDWOMEN

WESTERN LENS	MIDDLE EASTERN LENS
Form	Function
How? *How did it happen?*	Why? *Why would God do that?*
Understand → Believe	Believe → Understand
Law, Rule, Principle	Story, Narrative
What does it teach me about *me*?	What does it teach me about *God*?
Dig deep, get down in it . . . *(Analysis—pick it apart)*	Read through it . . . *(Synthesis—bring it together)*
Study to acquire *knowledge*	Posture to be *fed*

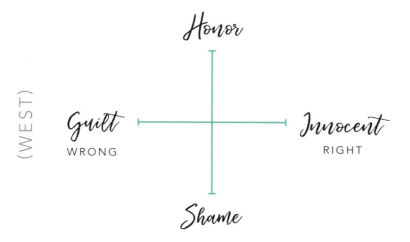

(MIDDLE EAST)

Honor

(WEST)

Guilt
WRONG

Innocent
RIGHT

Shame

YESHIVA

Each week we're going to take some time to *yeshiva*—to emulate the Middle Eastern communal way of discussing spiritual concepts and growing together in grace as a biblical community. Discuss the following questions with your group.

What did you just hear or see in our feast together that you want to remember?

In Jesus's world, rabbis and Pharisees often used parables as their primary teaching method. They would share their theologies not in terms of academic teaching—what we might think of as *systematic theology*—but through stories. Approximately one-third of Jesus's recorded words in the Gospels are in parabolic form.[1]

> *parabolē*—parable
> *parallēlos*—parallel

Parables were very common in Jesus's day. However, rabbis and Pharisees rarely used women as the subject matter of their parables or stories. Women were considered too lowly to communicate divine things. Parables and stories were almost always told in the masculine.

How do you think women in Jesus's day felt about that?

However, Jesus was extremely unique in that He often included women in His stories, parables, and ministry. In the Gospel of Luke, we see twenty-seven pairings of spiritual teachings and Jesus's actions (see chart on pp. 88–90).[2] It was not unusual for Jesus to share two stories or parables: one featuring a man, the other featuring a woman. With Jesus, women found their place in the story over and over again. Jesus brought a generous justice to women everywhere through the very way He shaped, formed, and taught His parables.

READ LUKE 18:1-8.

Who did Jesus choose to cast as the main character of this parable?

When Jesus wanted to teach a parable about praying with persistence, He could have used several historical and biblically important characters, for example:

- Abraham praying and contending for Sodom and Gomorrah (Gen. 18).
- Jacob wrestling with the angel of the Lord at the river Jabbok (Gen. 32).
- Moses praying for God's anger to turn from the idolatrous Israelites (Ex. 32).
- Hannah praying for a child during her years of barrenness (1 Sam. 1).

How does it make you feel to realize that Jesus was adamant about including women in His stories and parables?

What does this parable teach about prayer?

This widow began the story at the bottom, powerless against an unrighteous judge. But she ended the story on top, having bent the will of the unrighteous judge with her *chutzpah* (persistence in coming to him over and over again). [3]

How long do you tend to pray for something before you give up? Before you quit? Explain.

What would it look like for you to pray with *chutzpah*?

THE TEACHINGS OF JESUS

Jesus was adamant about including women. The following chart shows the way that Jesus made a point of including both women and men in His spiritual teachings and His earthly ministry, an unheard of practice in His day.

PAIRINGS IN THE GOSPEL OF LUKE

MASCULINE	FEMININE
Gabriel appears to Zechariah (1:8-23)	Gabriel appears to Mary (1:26-38)
Song of Zechariah (1:67-79)	Song of Mary (1:46-55)
Simeon encounters baby Jesus in the temple (2:25-35)	Anna encounters baby Jesus in the temple (2:36-38)
Naaman and Israelite lepers (4:27)	Widow of Zarephath and Israelite widows (4:25-26)
Healing of demon-possessed man in Capernaum (4:31-37)	Healing of Simon's mother-in-law in Capernaum (4:38-39)
The parable of new wine in new wineskins (5:37-39)	The parable of sewing a patch on old clothes (5:36)
Naming of twelve apostles (6:12-16)	Naming of the women who were with Jesus (8:1-3)
Centurion's servant healed (7:1-10)	Widow of Nain's son raised from the dead (7:11-17)
The parable of men who each owed a debt (7:41-43)	Jesus forgives a sinful woman (7:36-50)

MASCULINE	FEMININE
Jesus traveled with the Twelve (8:1)	Some women who'd been healed also traveled with Jesus (8:2)
Fear addressed—disciples in a boat during a storm (8:22-25)	Fear addressed—Jairus's daughter healed (8:41-42,49-56)
Healing of demon-possessed man in Gerasenes (8:26-39)	Healing of a bleeding woman (8:43-48)
The parable of the good Samaritan (10:25-37)	Example of Mary choosing to sit at Jesus's feet (10:38-42)
Family divided: father versus son (12:52-53)	Family divided: mother versus daughter (12:52-53)
Sick man healed (14:1-6)	Crippled woman healed (13:10-17)
The parable of a man planting a mustard seed (13:18-19)	The parable of a woman mixing yeast and flour (13:20-21)
The parable of the lost son (15:11-32)	The parable of the woman looking for a lost coin (15:8-10)
The parable of the shrewd manager taking advantage of position (16:1-15)	Teaching on divorce—men taking advantage of women (16:18)
Two men sleeping, one taken (17:34)	Two women grinding meal, one taken (17:35)
Rich young ruler won't receive kingdom (18:18-30)	(Likely) Women bringing children to Jesus—theirs is the kingdom (18:15-17)
The parable of the Pharisee and the tax collector—prayer (18:9-14)	The parable of the persistent widow—prayer (18:1-8)

MASCULINE	FEMININE
Rich Pharisees giving in the temple treasury (20:45–21:1)	The poor widow giving two copper coins (21:2-4)
Last days—men will faint from terror (21:26)	Last days—dreadful for nursing and pregnant mothers (21:23)
Two men question Peter (22:58-59)	Servant girl questions Peter (22:56-57)
Simon of Cyrene carries Jesus's cross (23:26)	Jesus meets women on way to Calvary (23:27-29)
Joseph of Arimathea buries Jesus's body (23:50-53)	Women see where Jesus is buried (23:55-56)
Resurrection evidence—two men on way to Emmaus (24:13-35)	Resurrection evidence—women see angels at empty tomb (24:1-8)

In the first-century world, before Jesus upended things, all spiritual teaching was for men. Imagine, as a woman, hearing the teaching of God's Word with your family, to only find spiritual application directed just at your male relatives. We have so much access to spiritual teaching today, it's easy to take it for granted. For a moment, though, put yourself in the shoes of a first-century Jewish woman.

What do you imagine it would have been like to have no spiritual teaching directed to you? How do you think it would have affected your spiritual growth and your attitude toward God?

In His approach to teaching and His earthly ministry, Jesus said to women in the first century—you are a part of this story, too. You matter. You're seen by God. You're prized by God. You're in His story. God is calling you to be a part of His kingdom work. And Jesus is saying that to us as women today, too.

The point of a parable is to drive you to a decision. In the parable of the persistent widow in Luke 18, for example, the text challenges our understanding of why and how we should pray. Parables are meant to spur action; again, here we see the Middle Eastern idea of obedience to God's Word through embodiment. We don't simply read His Word; we walk it out. We make His Word a part of who we are, so much so that it shapes the way we think and act day in and day out.

Pick two of the pairings in the chart on pages 88-90. As you read both passages in each pair, record below what you think the parables/stories teach and how the parables/stories impacts the way you live.

 PAIRING #1:

What the parables/stories teach:

How it impacts the way you live:

 PAIRING #2:

What the parables/stories teach:

How it impacts the way you live:

PERSONAL STUDY

Look

ZAKHAR

We have spiritual disciplines and practices as New Testament believers, certain things we do as Christians to live out our faith. When I hear the phrase *spiritual disciplines*, lots of things come to mind, such as Bible study, prayer, attending a local church, tithing, living missionally, and serving others.

Throughout time, the Jewish people have also had their own spiritual rhythms and practices. In the Bible we see God issue many commandments, but He repeats one of them over and over: *Remember. Do not forget.*

The Lord knows we are a forgetful people. I often forget where I put my car keys. I walk into a room sometimes and forget why I went there in the first

WE EASILY FORGET THE THINGS THE LORD HAS DONE FOR US—HIS FAITHFUL RECORD OVER THE COURSE OF OUR WHOLE LIVES.

place! Similarly, we tend to have spiritual amnesia. We easily forget the things the Lord has done for us—His faithful record over the course of our whole lives.

Instead, we tend to remember our traumas, our hurts, the things that have devastated us and left us reeling, trying to catch our breath. We often forget the blessings—the beautiful things and the grace-filled moments when the Lord has provided healing, restoration, redemption, grace, direction, or divine intervention.

The Hebrew word *zakhar* means "to remember."[4] We typically define "remembering" as looking back or thinking back to something in the past. But in the Hebrew culture, remembering is the way to move forward, to step into the unknown future. Biblical remembering, or *zakhar*, carries this same idea of forward motion.

Here's how it practically plays out: If you come to a place or a time when you aren't sure where to go or what to do next, pause and look back. Remember how the Lord met you, directed you, and provided for you in those past times.

Remembering God's faithful record in our lives gives us courage to trust Him in the unknown and live forward. We *zakhar* (remember) so that we can step forward, because the same God who was faithful to be with us in the past is the God who will be faithful to be with us in a future that may seem unknown.

We can practice *zakhar* both personally and communally. In the Jewish feasts and festivals, God prescribed corporate occasions for remembering. In these festivals, the Jewish people come together to remember and retell their God stories to their children and celebrate God's faithfulness in their lives and in their stories. Remembering always brings celebration because God has *never* failed us—His record is one hundred percent.

Take a moment to brainstorm and consider a few spiritual practices of remembering that you could add to your life, both on your own and with others. Record them below.

My personal remembering rhythm is journaling. My communal remembering rhythm is inviting people to come sit around my fire pit with me as we tell our God stories by firelight. Both practices allow me to rehearse telling the story of God's goodness and give Him glory in the seasons of ease and difficulty. Feel free to give them a try.

IT'S ALL ABOUT PERSPECTIVE

In Luke 15, Jesus shares a parable made up of three different stories. It's like a series of three pearls strung together to share the beautiful truth of how the Lord comes looking for us when we are lost, how He comes to bring us home. He truly comes to seek (go looking for) and save (bring home) the lost.

Throughout the history of the canon of Scripture, as the Bible was adapted into different languages and arranged, editors added chapter and verse labels, along with the subheading descriptions you see in your Bibles, to aid readers in locating and citing portions of the Scriptures.[5]

The subheadings and story titles often reflect our Western lens—one that asks, "What does this passage teach me about *me*?"

But, in the Middle East, the same passages of Scripture often have different subheadings and story titles, descriptions that reflect the Middle Eastern lens, asking, "What does this teach me about *God*?"

Let's use Luke 15 as an example of how our lens so often determines what we are looking for or focusing on in a passage of Scripture.

READ LUKE 15.

 *Look at this Bible passage through the **Western lens,** asking the question, "What does this teach me about **me**?" Write down what you notice in these stories.*

Look at this Bible passage through the Middle Eastern lens, asking the question, "What does this teach me about God?" Write down what you notice in these stories.

The chart below shows the subheadings that accompany these Luke 15 stories in a Western Bible versus the Middle Eastern text.

LUKE 15 DESCRIPTIONS

WEST	MIDDLE EAST
The parable of the lost sheep	The parable of the good shepherd
The parable of the lost coin	The parable of the good woman
The parable of the lost son [6]	The parable of the running father [7]

Would you rather read a story about a lost sheep or a good shepherd? Would you rather read a story about a lost coin or a good woman? Would you rather read a story about a lost son or a running father who goes to find his lost son?

Having read the passage, which of the descriptions resonates with you more?

Reading the Bible with a Middle Eastern lens helps us to learn to stare at God and glance at our lives. It prompts us to pivot our gaze and the focus of our hearts off of ourselves and circumstances and instead fix our eyes on God, His work, His faithfulness, His goodness, and His generous justice in our lives. Notice Jesus used a woman as the main character in the second story here in Luke 15. Her story sets up the famous parable of the prodigal son, or as I prefer to call it, the parable of the running father.

Live

YOUR GOD STORIES

Jesus loved using women in His stories and parables. He wanted to make sure women knew they had and have a place—an important place—in the story of the Bible and the redemptive, restorative flow of human history.

Your stories matter. Your story matters. The little stories and the big story. All of it. The up, down, and all around of your life. It all matters to Jesus. Since Jesus used women in His stories and parables, we should be women who share our stories to bless, encourage, edify, challenge, and strengthen others. Plus, our stories give glory to God. It's a win-win.

What are some of the most important God stories in your own life? Write one or two below.

Have you ever written them down before or shared them with other people? Why or why not?

What would it look like for you to both personally and communally *zakhar* (remember)?

Session Seven

JESUS AND THE WOMAN ON THE SOUTHERN STEPS

{ THE FEAST }

We are getting ready to pull up our chairs for Session Seven of this biblical feast prepared for us by our Father. He feeds. We receive. The Lord will take His Word and break it down for us today in bite-size pieces. We are a saved people. We are also a fed people.

BEGIN

As we begin our feast, take a few moments to answer the following questions before you watch the video teaching.

What have you been thinking about since last week's feast?

Who did you live like a river toward last week by sharing what you learned at the feast?

How did that conversation go? How did your time together challenge you or confirm what you've been learning?

Use the following space or the blank pages at the back of this book during our feast teaching time to add your own notes as you watch.

THE TEACHING SESSION BUNDLE IS AVAILABLE FOR PURCHASE AT LIFEWAY.COM/JESUSANDWOMEN

WESTERN LENS	MIDDLE EASTERN LENS
Form	Function
How? *How did it happen?*	Why? *Why would God do that?*
Understand → Believe	Believe → Understand
Law, Rule, Principle	Story, Narrative
What does it teach me about *me*?	What does it teach me about *God*?
Dig deep, get down in it . . . *(Analysis—pick it apart)*	Read through it . . . *(Synthesis—bring it together)*
Study to acquire *knowledge*	Posture to be *fed*

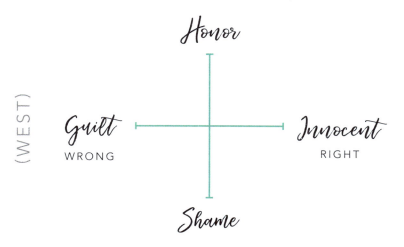

(MIDDLE EAST)

Honor

(WEST)

Guilt
WRONG

Innocent
RIGHT

Shame

YESHIVA

Each week we're going to take some time to *yeshiva*—to emulate the Middle Eastern communal way of discussing spiritual concepts and growing together in grace as a biblical community. Discuss the following questions with your group.

What did you just *hear* or *see* in our feast together that you want to remember?

This week, we see the epic love of Jesus for woman. It's an electric story that reaches deep, high, and wide in its scope. Today we see what Jesus would do with a sinful woman—a woman caught in adultery.

Read John 8:1-11 (NIV) below:

But Jesus went to the Mount of Olives. At dawn he appeared again in the temple courts, where all the people gathered around him, and he sat down to teach them. The teachers of the law and the Pharisees brought in a woman caught in adultery. They made her stand before the group and said to Jesus, "Teacher, this woman was caught in the act of adultery. In the Law Moses commanded us to stone such women. Now what do you say?" They were using this question as a trap, in order to have a basis for accusing him.

But Jesus bent down and started to write on the ground with his finger. When they kept on questioning him, he straightened up and said to them, "Let any one of you who is without sin be the first to throw a stone at her." Again he stooped down and wrote on the ground.

At this, those who heard began to go away one at a time, the older ones first, until only Jesus was left, with the woman still standing there. Jesus straightened up and asked her, "Woman, where are they? Has no one condemned you?"

"No one, sir," she said.

"Then neither do I condemn you," Jesus declared. "Go now and leave your life of sin."

The *first* time Jesus wrote in the sand (honoring Sabbath regulations about writing), scholars believe He most likely wrote out the words of Leviticus 20:10 in response to their question about the Law of Moses concerning adultery.[1]

> **"'If a man commits adultery with another man's wife—with the wife of his neighbor—both the adulterer and the adulteress are to be put to death.'"**
> LEVITICUS 20:10

The Pharisees brought in a woman caught in adultery. Where was the man? They weren't honestly concerned with the Law being broken, or they would have brought the man involved in the adultery, too. They were trying to trap Jesus in a public moment with lots of people around.

Jesus's next words were about who would stone the woman—the penalty for adultery in the Law of Moses. Jesus said the ones among them without sin should be first to throw a stone at her.

Is anyone on earth without sin? If not, who should have been left standing?

When Jesus started writing their names, the religious leaders began walking away. Jesus had shifted their wrath off of the woman and onto Himself. The Pharisees started out mad at her, and they walked away mad at Him for calling them out. Once they had all walked away, only Jesus and the woman were there.

What do you think the woman felt in that moment, standing alone with just Jesus?

In my opinion, whether she knew it or not, this was actually the scariest moment for the woman. Jesus was sinless. He was the only one who could have justly thrown the stone if He chose to do so.

How did Jesus bring a generous justice to the woman in this passage?

Jesus atoned for (covered) her sin, her shame, and generously lifted her up. He literally saved her life from the religious leaders who would certainly have stoned her to death if it were left up to them.

READ 2 CORINTHIANS 5:21.

Just like Jesus did for the woman caught in adultery, He took on your sin when He died on the cross. He endured the punishment that you deserved, and now He covers your shame. This story is a reminder that if He did it for her, He can do it for you.

Put yourself in the place of the woman. You don't have to answer out loud, but what is the sin in your life that causes you guilt and shame? What part of your life do you want to hide?

If you have never placed your hope or trust in Jesus, what's keeping you from calling out to Him to save you from your sin? Talk with your leader or trusted adult if you have questions about surrendering your life to Jesus.

Sin always has to be dealt with, and Jesus paid for it in full on the cross. Forgiveness and restoration are found in Him.

SHIFTING OUR GAZE

On any given day, we are usually spending most of our time staring at one thing and glancing at everything else in our lives. Something has our attention. Something is on our minds.

When we stare at our lives and glance at God, the troubles and problems in our lives can begin to look huge. If we're not careful, our problems take up most of the space in our thoughts and consequently govern our hearts and emotions.

When we intentionally focus our minds and hearts on God, our troubles take on their proper perspective. God helps us to see them in light of His generous justice, His generous lifting up in our lives.

WHEN WE INTENTIONALLY FOCUS OUR MINDS AND HEARTS ON GOD, OUR TROUBLES TAKE ON THEIR PROPER PERSPECTIVE.

What are you currently staring at in your life?

What troubles or problems seem huge as you stare at them?

What would it look like for you to consider that trouble, that problem, up against God—His love, power, and wisdom?

PERSONAL STUDY

WHERE JESUS WALKED

The Southern Rabbinic Teaching Steps

Our story this week almost certainly occurred on the Southern Rabbinic Teaching Steps at the temple in Jerusalem. Sometimes today these teaching steps are called the Southern Steps. If you go to Israel, you simply *must* go sit on those steps. Why?

You must visit them because Jesus walked these very steps, and He walked them often. It's one place where we *know* He spent time. So did Joseph, Mary, Peter, John, James, Stephen, Paul, Silas, Barnabas, Timothy, and many other people we read about in the pages of Scripture.

Three Annual Pilgrimage Festivals

> *Three times a year all your men must appear before the LORD your God at the place he will choose: at the Festival of Unleavened Bread [Passover], the Festival of Weeks [Pentecost] and the Festival of Tabernacles.*
> DEUTERONOMY 16:16a

In Torah, the Lord commanded the Jewish people to come to His house (temple) in Jerusalem three times a year for the festivals and feasts, also known as the *pilgrimage festivals* or *foot festivals*. We've talked about them briefly already.

In these seven-day festivals, Jewish people came to Jerusalem from all over to celebrate God's faithfulness *with* Him at His house. They collectively and communally remembered God's faithful provision for them over the past year and celebrated together.

As pilgrims arrived at the temple and ascended the Southern Steps, they possibly sang the psalms of ascent (Pss. 120–134) in anticipation of going into God's house to worship, remember, and celebrate together.[2] The steps were arranged in an irregular fashion, both the original stones and the stones that have been replaced since then. The height and width of the stairs were not consistent. They were specifically designed to make the pilgrim think and consider the solemnity of worship and going before God as they ascended to the Huldah Gates to enter the temple.

talmid

In the first-century world, a disciple (*talmid*) wanted to be just like his rabbi.[3] A *talmid* didn't want to know what his rabbi knew—the *talmid* wanted to *be like* the rabbi.

People chose their rabbis in Jesus's world. You would listen to a rabbi over time, and if you agreed with the way he interpreted Scripture and respected his leadership, you would ask if you could follow him—if you could be one of his *talmidim* (disciples).[4]

Jesus was revolutionary when He came on the scene because *He* reached out to certain people and chose *them* as His disciples. When He chose them, in the culture of the day He was implicitly saying, "I think you can be just like me."

Later, Jesus told His disciples they would do greater things than He had done (see John 14:12). How can this be? He knew they would go into the world in multiplied fashion, serving the world as His disciples—He knew they would go be just like Him as the Spirit of God enabled them throughout the world.

You can just imagine the way Jerusalem would have come alive during the three annual festivals—the hustle and bustle, the throngs of people, the chatter and laughter and merriment—a people celebrating the faithfulness of their God with Him at His house.

Daily Life on the Southern Steps in Jesus's First-Century World

The Southern Rabbinic Teaching Steps were also where Pharisees and rabbis taught their disciples (*talmidim*) during the first-century world of Jesus. Rabbis did not teach inside the temple. The temple was reserved for worship, prayer, and sacrifice. Teaching happened on the Southern Steps.

Rabbis and Pharisees also discussed, debated, and shared their teachings with one another on those steps. Remember, our story this week took place on the eighth day after the fall Festival of Tabernacles; everyone had been in Jerusalem for the foot festival. The day after the Festival of Tabernacles ended, Jesus went back to the temple to teach. [8]

> *Then they all went home, but Jesus went to the Mount of Olives. At dawn he appeared again in the temple courts, where all the people gathered around him, and he sat down to teach them. The teachers of the law and the Pharisees brought in a woman caught in adultery.*
> JOHN 7:53–8:3a

Jesus was probably sitting on the Southern Steps, teaching His *talmidim* (disciples) when the religious leaders brought in a woman caught in the act of adultery.

READ JOHN 8:3-11.

Every time I sit on those steps, I think of her. What she must have experienced that day some two thousand years ago—the public humiliation, her sin named out loud for all the pilgrims to hear. Her terror, because she knew the penalty for adultery in her world was stoning. She probably believed she wouldn't see the sun set that night. I wonder while she stood there, taking it all in, taking it in for what might possibly be the last time: What was she thinking about? Her family? Her children? How badly the rocks would hurt hitting her hard as they were hurled down at her? I wonder what her prayer sounded like in that moment.

But Jesus atoned for (covered) her, generously lifted her up out of her sin and shame and sent her away in peace—encouraging her to live forward in a new way.

> **_Go now and leave your life of sin._**
> JOHN 8:11b

What about this story in John 8 fuels your worship of Jesus?

Neil Armstrong, the first man to ever step foot onto the moon, visited Israel one year and went to the Southern Steps. When he learned that Jesus had walked on those very steps so often during His earthly life and ministry, Armstrong said, "I am more excited stepping on these stones than I was stepping on the moon."[6]

Yarah

When we see the word *law*, it can bring up thoughts of rules and regulations—things we are penalized for if we break them (think of something like a speeding ticket).

The word *law* in the Old Testament is the Hebrew word *yarah*. Contrary to our Western idea of law, the word *yarah* carries the idea of instructions.

God's laws are His instructions. Instructions for what?

For how to live in *shalom*.

God gives us instructions to help us hit the mark, to live in *shalom*—the abundant life He desires for us.

We might shy away from *law*, but we love *instructions* for living in *shalom*. This was the psalmist's delight in Psalm 119, as they wrote about their love for the laws of God, because His laws show us the path for flourishing that He has mapped out for us.

Learn

SEEKING SHALOM

Our story this week ends with Jesus sending the woman caught in adultery away, generously lifting her up with the encouragement to go and leave her life of sin.

How would you define "sin"?

In essence, sin means to "miss the mark."[7] It's an archery term. The laws of God help us to hit the mark. The Hebrew word for "law" in the Old Testament is *yarah,* and it means "instructions."[8] God gives us instructions in His laws. Instructions for what? What mark are we trying to hit? What mark do we miss when we sin?

When you sin or break the law/yarah of the Lord, how do you feel?

We often think of the opposite of sin as righteousness or cleanness. This is a right understanding, so we want to hang onto it. While keeping this understanding in mind, we also want to expand our understanding and look at these things in the greater meta-narrative, or flow, of the big story of the Bible.

The garden of Eden was created in *shalom*, a Hebrew word that means wholeness, harmony, flourishing, and delight.[9] Most people hear the word *shalom* and immediately think of peace. But in Hebrew, *shalom* means much more than peace.

In Genesis 3, Adam and Eve ate the forbidden fruit and sin entered the world, the Story. *Shalom* was disturbed and thrown off balance because sin messes up the way things were meant to be. We were created for Eden but find ourselves living in a broken world, where sin still disturbs *shalom*.

The opposite of sin is *shalom*—the way God created things to be. The Lord doesn't hate sin because we broke a rule, law, or instruction; the Lord hates sin because sin disturbs our *shalom*. It disrupts our harmony, wholeness, flourishing, delight, and communion with God. It disrupts the way God created us to be—in relationship with Him and with one another. In encouraging the woman in our story this week to leave her life of sin, Jesus was inviting her into *shalom*—a renewed sense of the harmony, wholeness, flourishing, and delight the Lord wished for her to know and experience in her life.

> Now that you've most likely heard me talk about *shalom* in a new way, describe it below in your own words.

> How does confession and repentance move you back toward *shalom*?

READ JOHN 21:4-19.

 *Look at this Bible passage through the **Western lens**, asking the question, "What does this teach me about **me**?" (This would cause us to focus on Peter in the story.) Write down what you notice in this story.*

You may remember the following part of Peter's story: Jesus prophesied that Peter would deny any affiliation with Jesus among the crowds before His crucifixion. Though Peter vehemently asserted he would never do such a thing, we see him deny Jesus three times in John 18, just as Jesus foretold. In the John 21 passage that we just read, we believe we're reading the account of Peter seeing the resurrected Jesus for the third time.

Many scholars believe John 21 took place in a location in Israel that is now called "the Primacy of Peter," a place where waterfalls come together into springs. Jewish fishermen often used this location to wash their nets. We also believe that this location is where Jesus called Peter and his brother Andrew to follow Him in the first place.[10] If that's true, we imagine this location must have held some significant memories for Peter. Fishing there, he may have remembered the day that Jesus, one of the most famous rabbis, chose him. With those happy memories would have likely come a pang of guilt and anxiety about betraying Jesus.

Peter saw Jesus, who called him and chose him, and whom Peter rejected. Then, that same Jesus, who called Peter to follow Him those years ago, called Peter to the table, a place of restoration, a place of communal love and affiliation.

Jesus meets us where we are and never leaves us there.

We may all have a moment like this with Jesus one day, a moment where we know we've blown it and Jesus graciously restores our fellowship with Him—moving us forward into *shalom*, moving us forward into purpose for Him. When we come to Jesus, we lose our lives as we know them, but God just keeps giving more and more. He keeps generously lifting us up to love and know Him. God is better than we ever knew.

If you desire for Jesus to restore you today, spend some time in prayer confessing your need for Him.

EPIC LOVE

Everything about this week's biblical story is epic—the public nature of the incident, the fact that it happened in Jerusalem the day after a seven-day festival, the intent of the religious leaders to lay a trap for Jesus, the grave nature of the woman's sin with a penalty of stoning in the Torah, and the fact that Jesus was sitting on the Southern Steps teaching His disciples when the religious leaders brought the sinful woman before Him.

Jesus's love for the woman was also epic. He shifted the wrath of the Pharisees off of her and turned it onto Himself—to the point that they walked away mid-story, mid-moment. Jesus atoned for (covered) the woman's sin and shame; He saved her life and sent her away in peace.

The love God has for you is epic. If you are a follower of Christ, He has shifted the wrath of your enemies onto Himself, atoned for your sin and shame, and sent you away in peace—to walk the path of *shalom* in renewed life and service to Him, much as He did for this woman.

What have been the most epic moments of your life?

Is there anything disturbing you**r** *shalom* right now? Explain.

Do not be afraid to name the thing disturbing your *shalom* and confess it to Jesus. His love for you is epic—He will cover, forgive, and send you forward in *shalom*. He will generously lift you up.

Session Eight

JESUS
AND THE
TALE
OF TWO
MARYS

{ THE FEAST }

We are getting ready to pull up our chairs for our final session of this biblical feast. We are getting ready to eat the biblical meal prepared for us by our Father. He feeds. We receive. The Jewish people read the Scriptures over and over again. In the same way we don't eat one meal and then never eat again, we eat the Scriptures over and over again.

BEGIN

As we begin our feast, take a few moments to answer the following questions before you watch the video teaching.

What have you been thinking about since last week's feast?

Who did you live like a river toward last week by sharing what you learned at the feast?

How did that conversation go? How did your time together challenge you or confirm what you've been learning?

Use the following space or the blank pages at the back of this book during our feast teaching time to add your own notes as you watch.

THE TEACHING SESSION BUNDLE IS AVAILABLE FOR PURCHASE AT LIFEWAY.COM/JESUSANDWOMEN

WESTERN LENS	MIDDLE EASTERN LENS
Form	Function
How? *How did it happen?*	Why? *Why would God do that?*
Understand → Believe	Believe → Understand
Law, Rule, Principle	Story, Narrative
What does it teach me about *me*?	What does it teach me about *God*?
Dig deep, get down in it . . . *(Analysis—pick it apart)*	Read through it . . . *(Synthesis—bring it together)*
Study to acquire *knowledge*	Posture to be *fed*

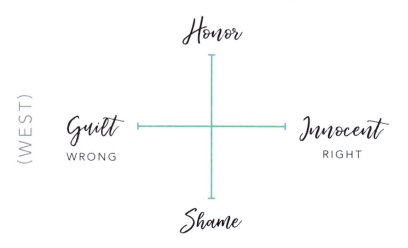

(MIDDLE EAST)

Honor

(WEST)

Guilt
WRONG

Innocent
RIGHT

Shame

YESHIVA

Each week we're going to take some time to *yeshiva*—to emulate the Middle Eastern communal way of discussing spiritual concepts and growing together in grace, as a biblical community. Discuss the following questions with your group.

What did you just *hear* or *see* in our feast together that you want to remember?

This week we will see what are, in my opinion, one of the hardest *yes*es a person in the Bible ever gave to the Lord and one of the most unique *yes*es a person in the Bible ever gave to Jesus. Spoiler alert: they were both given by women! We will also head toward the finish line for our series by looking at how we can take heart today as God's daughters and live our lives from that posture.

READ LUKE 1:26-38.

Imagine yourself in Mary's place in this story. What is going through your mind right after the angel tells you that you are pregnant with the Son of the Most High?

How does Mary's response make you feel? Do you think your response would be similar?

What has been one of the hardest *yes*es you have ever given to the Lord? Describe the situation.

One of the most unique *yes*es in the Bible belonged to another Mary (Miriam)—Mary the sister of Lazarus and Martha. She very well might have been the woman against the wall in our Luke 7 story. She might have been the one to bring the alabaster jar and tear jar to Simon's home.

READ LUKE 10:38-42.

Who do you compare yourself to more in this passage: Martha or Mary? Why?

The disciple (*talmid*) relationship with a rabbi was very important in the first-century world of Jesus. *Talmidim* didn't just want to know what their rabbi knew—they wanted to be like him. A disciple followed so closely to the rabbi that the dust of his feet got on him or her. A disciple didn't want any of the rabbi's words to "fall to the ground." "Sitting at the feet" of a rabbi was a formal term in the first century. Recognized disciples (*talmidim*) "sat at the feet" of their rabbis.

In Luke 10, Jesus was visiting Lazarus, Martha, and Mary. He started teaching. Mary "sat at the Lord's feet" (v. 39) learning, asking questions, interacting with the others.

What does this imply about Mary in this passage?

What was her unique *yes* in this passage?

What has been one of the most unique *yes*es you have ever given to the Lord? Describe the situation.

Why is Jesus always worth saying "yes" to?

Is the Lord bringing an adventure to you right now in this season of your life? (I think He is bringing adventures into each of our lives.) What is it?

How can this group come alongside you as you say "yes" to this kingdom adventure?

We serve a living God. And we have a living hope. And when He is handing out some of His kingdom adventures, they are going to come to you—even as girls. Will you be fully alive, fully awake, and ready, by faith and in faith in Him, to say "yes"?

If we've learned anything at all about Jesus in His first century Jewish world, it's that He is for women. He is a friend to women.

MARY–MIRIAM

This week's feast focused on two women, both named Mary. I like to call this week's teaching "The Tale of Two Marys." However, Mary isn't a Jewish name. Mary is the anglicized version of the Hebraic name Miriam.

The Jewish people are a deeply historical people. As a people, they intentionally remember, look back at their history as a people and what God has done for them, and take courage to live forward. Children were often named after the "greats" in Israel's history. Both Marys in our stories today, both Miriams, were named after the Miriam of the Old Testament—the sister of Moses and Aaron.[1]

Miriam was born to Amram and Jochebed during the Hebrews' enslavement to the Egyptians. She was born before Aaron and Moses.[2] The name Miriam means "bitterness,"[3] a sentiment that illustrated life under Egyptian rule and oppression.[4] We see Miriam acting in great faith when she followed Moses in the basket as it made its way down the Nile River. When Pharaoh's daughter found him, Miriam approached her and offered a Jewish wet nurse to care for baby Moses. Pharaoh's daughter said *yes*, and Miriam went and got Jochebed, Moses's mother (see Ex. 2).

Later, Miriam came to be known as a prophetess among the Israelites (see Ex. 15:20).

READ EXODUS 15.

Moses and Miriam's song is recorded in Exodus 15 after the miraculous crossing of the Red Sea by the Israelites. She was a faithful daughter and sister in a season of peril and deliverance for the Israelites. She was a prophetess to her people—a prophetess with powerful words.

What Jewish girl wouldn't want to be named after such an incredible woman in Jewish history?

Take a moment to consider the type of life you're leading. Is it marked by courage and trust in God? Or more trust in yourself? What do you want to be known for at the end of your life? Record your thoughts below or in a journal.

{ PERSONAL STUDY }

Before You Start: Grab your highlighters or colored pens! We want you to engage as you read, so choose your colors to mark meaningful quotes and insights.

- ☐ Use this color to <u>underline</u> something new you've learned.
- ☐ Use this color to ⟨circle⟩ something you don't want to forget.
- ☐ Use this color to *star* something you need to live out.

Look

KINGDOM ADVENTURES

READ LUKE 1:26-56.

"I am the Lord's servant," Mary answered, "May your word to me be fulfilled." Then the angel left her. At that time Mary got ready and hurried to a town in the hill country of Judea, where she entered Zechariah's home and greeted Elizabeth.
LUKE 1:38-40

We wonder how many people in Nazareth—if any at all—would have believed Mary when they heard this story. Even her husband-to-be didn't believe her at first. Joseph was preparing to "divorce her quietly" when an angel visited him in a dream to tell him it was true (see Matt. 1:19-25). If Joseph had trouble getting his head and heart around this news, it's easy to imagine the greater community and village not being able to get their heads or hearts around it at all.

A betrothed, not-yet-married girl showing up pregnant? Mary lived in an honor/shame culture where women were stoned for such things. Mary "got ready and hurried" (v. 39). How far did she go? Not down the street. Not over two villages. She traveled all the way from the northern district of Galilee to the southern district of Judea. She went to Elizabeth's home, the home of her cousin.

Tradition places the home of Zechariah and Elizabeth in a tiny village called Ein Kerem, a village just southwest of historical Jerusalem. *Ein Kerem* means "spring of the vineyard." It is also where traditional says John the Baptist was born.

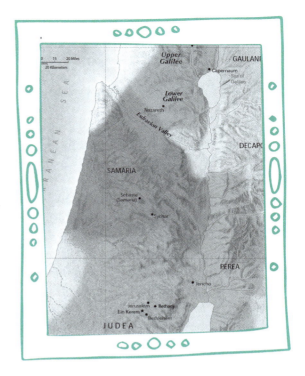

It was more than an eighty-mile journey from Nazareth to Ein Kerem. Mary was of the peasant class, so she probably didn't ride a donkey those eighty miles. Instead, we can imagine her walking with a caravan of fellow travelers as they made their way south to Jerusalem.

Mary, as a young betrothed girl, had been minding her own business one day when Gabriel showed up out of nowhere and invited her into the adventure of a lifetime. She had no idea what it would cost her, but she did know it could cost her life. She also knew she and Jesus would probably always live with some kind of social stigma regarding His legitimacy and the true story behind her pregnancy. We are forever grateful she said *yes* to the adventure that came to her.

When the Living God wants to hand out kingdom adventures, some of them are coming to girls, to women, to us! We don't need to go find kingdom adventures—they have a way of finding us.

If God were to approach you with a new kingdom adventure today, is there anything that would keep you from saying *yes* to Him? Explain.

CHOOSING WHAT IS BETTER

As Jesus and his disciples were on their way, he came to a village where a woman named Martha opened her home to him. She had a sister called Mary, who sat at the Lord's feet listening to what he said. But Martha was distracted by all the preparations that had to be made. She came to him and asked, "Lord, don't you care that my sister has left me to do the work by myself? Tell her to help me!" "Martha, Martha," the Lord answered, "you are worried and upset about many things, but few things are needed—or indeed only one. Mary has chosen what is better, and it will not be taken from her."
LUKE 10:38-42

 *Look at this Bible passage through the **Western lens,** the framework of understanding first and allowing that understanding to fuel belief. Write down what you notice in this story.*

 *Look at this Bible passage through the **Middle Eastern lens,** the framework of believing first and allowing that belief to fuel understanding. Write down what you notice in this story.*

Mary sat at the feet of Jesus, listening and learning as He taught His disciples. If you wait to understand everything about this passage to believe it, you might never move forward. However, if you take the Word as is and let it settle in your

heart, you will begin to move forward with new perspective, fresh insight, and quickened living.

 *Look at this Bible passage through the **Western lens**, asking the question, "What does this teach me about **me**?" Write down what you notice in this story.*

 *Look at this Bible passage through the **Middle Eastern lens**, asking the question, "What does this teach me about **God**?" Write down what you notice in this story.*

 *Look at this Bible passage through the **Middle Eastern lens**, asking the question, "What does this teach me about **Jesus**?" Write down what you notice in this story.*

Which perspective encourages you more, generously lifts you up more? Explain.

WALKING FORWARD

We have come to the end of our eight-week feast together. Much has been taught and shared in the teaching times. Much has been taught and shared in our times of *yeshiva*. We've been learning to take off our Western lenses and put on our Middle Eastern lenses when we read and *eat* the Bible. We've been learning that Jesus is better than we ever knew!

We've spent eight weeks learning to stare at God and glance at our lives. We've been learning to posture ourselves to receive, to be *fed* the Word of God by our Father. We've been living like rivers and not lakes, giving what we've been getting in our times together in the Scriptures to others. The Spirit of God takes the Word and feeds the women of God for the work of God. The Scriptures are living and active—we are living too. God-breathed life in the Word has been meeting our Spirit-quickened hearts, and we are better for having spent these eight weeks together.

We've been getting to know Jesus in His Jewish, first-century world. We've also been getting to know woman in her Jewish, first-century world. We've watched Jesus relate to a diverse grouping of women (Samaritan, Jewish, widow, adulteress) time and again with a unified sense of posture and purpose. Jesus moved toward them; He was for them and with them. He was working toward a deep and an ancient restoration as He brought *mishpat* (justice) and *tzedakah* (righteousness)—a generous lifting up to each one. Jesus's love is kind, fierce, unprecedented, and epic.

Jesus did not come to turn things upside down. He came to turn things right side up. The goal of every rabbi was to teach his disciples (*talmidim*) how to *halakh* (walk) the *halakha* (way or path) of God—the path of *shalom*. Jesus intended for women everywhere to live generously lifted up. If He did it for them, He can certainly do it for us today.

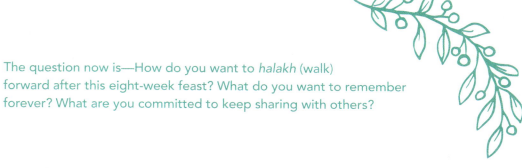

The question now is—How do you want to *halakh* (walk) forward after this eight-week feast? What do you want to remember forever? What are you committed to keep sharing with others?

Write down your main takeaways from this eight-week feast.

Write down your main commitments in the way you *halakh* (walk) forward with your life.

How do you want to live differently after sharing in this eight-week feast?

What would it look like for you to live more intentionally as one who is being generously lifted up by Jesus each and every day?

Wrap-up

CELEBRATION

In the West, we don't always know how to end something. But I say we should end in celebration. As a people who believe God is in the business of restoring the world to peace with Him, followers of Jesus Christ should be a people of celebration. The way we celebrate shows what we think about God.

In the Hebrew culture, people practice two fundamental spiritual rhythms (among others)—remembering and celebrating. These spiritual rhythms have changed my life. We've already talked about *zakhar*—remembering—a bit. But we've yet to discuss celebration as a spiritual rhythm.

I believe God put these spiritual practices before His people because He knows that we are a forgetful people. We tend to most easily forget the faithfulness of the Lord in our lives, because life kicks us all in the gut. The pain of the immediate can make it harder to remember what He has done and the promise of what He will do for us. These rhythms of remembering and celebrating anchor us in reality. We need them because so often how we're feeling isn't faithful to the truth of who God is. Remembering takes us back to the actual historical record of who God is and how He hasn't failed us yet—nor will He ever fail us.

There's something about remembering by actively celebrating that moves us forward—encouraged, emboldened, and courageous enough to lean into the thing in front of us. In the West, we think of memory as just looking back, but for the Hebrew people, it's a looking back to look forward. When we remember God's faithful record, both in our lives and in the family of God past and present, it quickens a sense of celebration in us because it reminds us of the eternal over the temporal. It reminds us of resurrection swallowing death. It reminds us God is going to see the story all the way through, shepherding us and this whole crazy world back to *shalom*.

We're going to live forever, in perfect *shalom* with God. Celebration connects us to the everyday reality that a deep and ancient restoration and renewal of all things is happening, even now in the midst of the mundane.

Pausing to reconnect with the meta-narrative of the Bible moves us forward. It quickens us to think again and anew: *If this is who God is, then who do I want to be?* So let's take a few minutes to consider, remember, celebrate, and move forward, eager to witness God's restoration in us and around us. Remembering and celebrating are some of the ways we take heart as daughters. Remember who God is; root your courage in His faithful character. Celebrate His love for you.

What could these rhythms of remembering and celebrating look like in your life? In your personal time with God? In your family or community of faith?

In light of everything we have learned about Jesus, who do you want to be? How do you want to live your life? Do you want to live it differently from how you did before this? Explain your thoughts.

How can you become someone who remembers and celebrates God's goodness to you? Below, or in a journal, take a few minutes to practice these spiritual rhythms. Remember by recording a few ways you've seen God be faithful in your life.

Leader Guide

LEADER TIPS

PRAY: Set aside time each week to pray for the girls in your group. Listen to their needs and the struggles they're facing so you can bring those needs before the Lord. Also make sure you prioritize your own personal time of prayer before each gathering. Encourage girls to include prayer as part of their own daily spiritual discipline as well.

GUIDE: Accept girls where they are, but also set expectations to motivate their commitment. Be consistent and trustworthy. Encourage girls to engage with the personal study and attend the group sessions. Listen carefully, responsibly guide discussion, and keep confidences shared within the group. Be honest and vulnerable by sharing what God is teaching you throughout the study. Most girls will follow your lead and be more willing to share and participate when they see your transparency.

CONNECT: Stay engaged with the girls in your group between group meetings. Call, text, or use social media to connect with them and share prayer needs throughout the week. Let them know when you are praying specifically for them. Root everything in Scripture, and encourage girls in their relationships with Jesus.

PLAN AND PREPARE: Visit lifeway.com/jesusandwomen to find free promotional resources for your study. Prepare an outline based on this Leader Guide to aid you as you lead the group discussion. Complete the personal study and group guide before each session, and be ready to share what you have learned to encourage girls to open up and discuss.

EVALUATE: At the end of each group session, ask yourself: *What went well? What could be improved? Did I see girls' lives transformed? Did my group grow closer to Christ and to one another?*

CELEBRATE: At the end of the study, celebrate what God has done by leading your group members to share what they've learned and how they've grown. Pray together about what further steps God may be asking you to take as a result of this study.

LOOKING FOR SOCIAL ASSETS TO SHARE WITH YOUR GIRLS? SCAN THIS QR CODE

SESSION ONE

FUN IDEA: Since it's your first week together, introduce the idea of "feast" by having your group time around a table (or tables). You might provide a meal or snacks for the girls to enjoy together. This is an idea you can use every week!

1. Welcome girls to the study, and distribute Bible study books. Use the *Begin* questions found in the *Feast* section (pp. 12–13) to get the conversation going.

2. Watch the Session One video, encouraging the girls to take notes as Kristi teaches.

3. Following the video, lead girls through the *Yeshiva* group discussion questions (pp. 14–17).

4. Remind the girls that there is no personal study to complete before next week. However, encourage them to get familiar with their Bible study book and to bring it back with them next week.

5. Close the session with prayer.

SESSION TWO

1. Welcome the girls to Session Two of *Jesus and Women*. Use the *Begin* questions found in the *Feast* section (pp. 20–21) to get the conversation going.

2. Watch the Session Two video, encouraging the girls to take notes as Kristi teaches.

3. Following the video, lead girls through the *Yeshiva* group discussion questions (pp. 22–25).

4. Remind the girls to complete the personal study on pages 26–35 at home on their own this week before you meet again.

5. Close the session with prayer.

SESSION THREE

1. Welcome the girls to Session Three of *Jesus and Women*. Use the *Begin* questions found in the *Feast* section (pp. 38–39) to get the conversation going.

2. Watch the Session Three video, encouraging the girls to take notes as Kristi teaches.

3. Following the video, lead girls through the *Yeshiva* group discussion questions (pp. 40–43).

4. Remind the girls to complete the personal study on pages 44–51 at home on their own this week before you meet again.

5. Close the session with prayer.

SESSION FOUR

1. Welcome the girls to Session Four of *Jesus and Women*. Use the *Begin* questions found in the *Feast* section (pp. 54–55) to get the conversation going.

2. Watch the Session Four video, encouraging the girls to take notes as Kristi teaches.

3. Following the video, lead girls through the *Yeshiva* group discussion questions (pp. 56–59).

4. Remind the group members to complete the personal study on pages 60–65 at home on their own this week before you meet again.

5. Close the session with prayer.

SESSION FIVE

1. Welcome the girls to Session Five of *Jesus and Women*. Use the *Begin* questions found in the *Feast* section (pp. 68–69) to get the conversation going.

2. Watch the Session Five video, encouraging the girls to take notes as Kristi teaches.

3. Following the video, lead girls through the *Yeshiva* group discussion questions (pp. 70–73).

4. Remind the group members to complete the personal study on pages 74–81 at home on their own this week before you meet again.

5. Close the session with prayer.

SESSION SIX

1. Welcome the girls to Session Six of *Jesus and Women*. Use the *Begin* questions found in the *Feast* section (pp. 84–85) to get the conversation going.

2. Watch the Session Six video, encouraging the girls to take notes as Kristi teaches.

3. Following the video, lead girls through the *Yeshiva* group discussion questions (pp. 86–91).

4. Remind the group members to complete the personal study on pages 92–97 at home on their own this week before you meet again.

5. Close the session with prayer.

SESSION SEVEN

1. Welcome the girls to Session Seven of *Jesus and Women*. Use the *Begin* questions found in the *Feast* section (pp. 100–101) to get the conversation going.

2. Watch the Session Seven video, encouraging the girls to take notes as Kristi teaches.

3. Following the video, lead girls through the *Yeshiva* group discussion questions (pp. 102–105).

4. Remind the group members to complete the personal study on pages 106–113 at home on their own this week before you meet again.

5. Close the session with prayer.

SESSION EIGHT

1. Welcome the girls to Session Eight of *Jesus and Women*. Use the *Begin* questions found in the *Feast* section (pp. 116–117) to get the conversation going.

2. Watch the Session Eight video, encouraging the girls to take notes as Kristi teaches.

3. Following the video, lead girls through the *Yeshiva* group discussion questions (pp. 118–121).

4. Remind the group members to complete the personal study on pages 122–127 at home on their own this week before you meet again.

5. Close the session with prayer.

WRAP UP CELEBRATION

This section can be used as an optional Session Nine if you would like one more group meeting, or you can choose to combine this with Session Eight. Even though you might have had snacks or meals provided each week, choose to do something special with your group to celebrate. You could have every girl bring a dish, you could dress up the table a bit more (think fancy!), or you could meet together at a restaurant. Ask your group how they want to celebrate the close of this study together and encourage them to take the lead.

However you choose to end your time together, make sure to encourage your girls to answer the discussion questions on their own as a way to reflect and celebrate all they accomplished as a group together.

Mom & Daughter

GUIDE

HEY, MOM!

We are so excited that you have decided to complete this study with your daughter. Kristi McLelland is going to walk you through a historical and biblical understanding of Jesus's relationship with women. We believe this will not only enrich your daughter's trust in the Lord, but we know it will strengthen your own love for Him, as well. What a beautiful thing for you to do together!

YOU WILL NEED

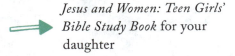

Jesus and Women: Women's Bible Study Book for yourself (with video access code)

Jesus and Women: Teen Girls' Bible Study Book for your daughter

Jesus and Women: Teen Girls' Video Bundle

PURCHASE THESE RESOURCES AT LIFEWAY.COM/JESUSANDWOMEN

VIDEO CONTENT

While the women's study of *Jesus and Women* includes video content of its own, we strongly encourage you to use the teen girl video bundle to go through this study with your daughter (purchased separately). These videos are teachings that Kristi adapted from the women's videos, but are shortened (approx. 15 minutes each) and designed to intentionally relate to the experiences of teen girls. The shorter videos allow for more discussion time, which can be found under *Yeshiva* in the teen girls Bible study book.

The videos included with the Women's Bible study book can still be viewed for your personal study. They will only strengthen the time you spend in the *Feast* and *Yeshiva* sections with your daughter.

PLEASE NOTE: *Jesus and Women: Teen Girls* is broken down into eight sessions, whereas there are only seven sessions in the *Jesus and Women* adult study. Due to the importance and the length of the content in Session One of the women's version, we decided it would be better to split this content into the first two sessions for teen girls.

STUDY

As you get started, use the content found in the *Feast* and *Yeshiva* sections of the teen girls' Bible study book for Session One. Personal Study will begin after you meet for Session Two.

As you both work through your individual Bible study books, you will discover that the teen girls' version might be slightly different, as we altered some language and content to be more applicable for teen girls. However, there are very few differences in the studies, and we encourage you to discuss what the Lord is teaching you individually.

CONNECT WITH HER

Plan days to work on Personal Study together to keep each other accountable. Be open with your daughter throughout the week about things you learn or have questions about. Provide a safe place for her to do the same. Don't stress! Accomplishing the Personal Study will be easier on some weeks than on others. Just keep pressing forward and making it a priority to meet together each week, regardless of how much personal study work was actually done.

FAQ

Q: How old does my teen need to be for this study?

A: This study is recommended for girls ages 11 and up.

Q: Are there other studies I can do with my daughter after this study is over?

A: Yes! Many of our studies have both women's and teen girls' materials available.

Glossary

BEN SIRA/SIRACH (PERSON): Originally from Jerusalem, Joshua son of Sira (or Yeshua Ben Sira) was a scribe who started a Jewish school in (presumably) Alexandria, Egypt, around 200 BC. Ben Sira was very knowledgeable of both Scripture (what he considered Scripture is now known as our Old Testament) and the human condition. However, his teachings were characterized by harsh treatment of both slaves and women—he considered them mere possessions to be handled however one wanted. These teachings were difficult to fathom in his day and are even more so in our own.[1]

THE BOOK OF BEN SIRA/SIRACH: Though numerous titles exist for this book of wisdom literature composed in the second century BC, it's most commonly known as *Ecclesiasticus* or *Sirach*. Ben Sira wrote the text in Hebrew originally, and decades later his grandson translated it to Greek. Though not considered canon by Protestants, both Catholic and Orthodox traditions deem it Scripture and include it in their list of Deuterocanonical works or Apocrypha. In content, it's most akin to the genre of wisdom literature as it contains numerous proverbs and ethical teachings.[2]

CULTURAL CONSIDERATIONS: As we approach the Bible with a new Middle Eastern lens, it's important to understand some significant differences between our culture today and the cultures of the first-century world. Though our cultural heritage and worldviews are valid, we in the 21st century approach the Bible in three vastly different ways than people two thousand years ago would have approached the Scripture.

First, we live in an innocence/guilt culture. This carries significance in the way we process sin as well as how we implement justice. (We know the drill: "Innocent until proven guilty," and "Let your conscience be your guide.") What happens, however, when justice cannot be found? Or when justice is faulty? To what point do we trust our consciences when we've seared them to such a degree that we no longer feel guilty when we do something wrong?

In the Middle East, they view the world differently. They function on an honor/shame continuum. In this culture, because everything centered on the family—religion, rituals, and politics—every member of that family carries the responsibility of bringing honor to their relatives. Shame is a reproach, and it comes in many forms. For example, cheating another family in a business transaction, being barren, and maintaining inappropriate relationships all bring shame on the rest of the family. On the other hand, fulfilling one's role as a daughter or son, wife or husband, priest or ruler brings honor. As a member of a family unit, everything one does either brings honor or shame, and in regards to sin and justice, all of it is connected to honor and shame.

This leads us to our second significant cultural difference. We emphasize the individual, but Middle Easterners two thousand years ago were all about the community. Notice how crucial this is to our understanding of the cultural difference we just discussed—innocence/guilt and honor/shame. In an individualistic culture like ours, sin is a private matter, lodged inside of us, and, therefore, sin is somewhat relative. What might be a sin for you, may not be for me; my weaknesses and strengths are different than yours. In a communal culture, however, everyone understands what is expected, and few things are done in secret. Even David, when he took in Bathsheba, was warned by his servants of who she was—someone else's wife! When living in community, sin is worn on the sleeve. Everyone knows what is happening, and a person's actions either bring shame or honor to their community.

Last, ancient (and present) Middle Eastern culture is highly hospitable, and I'm not just talking about having people over for some afternoon tea on the front porch. Hospitality was and is considered one of the greatest virtues one can express. If a stranger comes up to your house, or is simply walking nearby, you must invite them in. And when you do invite them in, your guests receive nothing but your absolute best! If you've been planning a special birthday party for a child, that visitor gets the party. If you've been saving for that new car, a large percentage of those savings goes to the guest in the form of food and entertainment. In certain nomadic cultures today, a family is required by custom and tradition to offer you their best food and drink for three days. It does not matter if you are Jewish, Muslim, Christian, Hindu, or Taoist. If you pass by or seek shelter in their dwelling, they will care for you as an honored guest.

CULTURAL IDIOMS: Within any language, we find nuance and cultural understanding that many times cannot be grasped by the simple definition of individual words within a phrase. If I say, "I'm in hot water," I'm not communicating I'm sitting in boiling water. Instead, I simply mean I'm in trouble. Other examples include: "They let the cat out of the bag," "It's raining cats and dogs," and "Break a leg." We have similar phrases in the Bible. But because we don't know the language and culture well, we often lose these phrases in translation or interpretive reading. For example, in the context of the Bible, having a "good eye" means being generous;[3] "to hear" means to literally hear but also to obey;[4] and "stiff-necked" means stubborn.[5] Some idioms have carried over to us in English, but there are many that remain unclear even to translators.

DAVAR: In English, one meaning of *davar* is "word." In this case, Hebrew speakers use the same noun as a verb too, so *davar* means not only "word," but also "he speaks." In fact, one of the many things that makes the Hebrew language of the Old Testament so fascinating is that words can carry multiple meanings—even in the same verse or phrase. For example, *davar* can also be translated as "thing."[6]

Because of this close connection between words and objects, religious Jews in the ancient world chose their words very carefully. (This is still true today.) They rarely, if ever, gossip. They call it "an evil tongue." Why? Because words carry weight. What and how we speak of ourselves and others matters. For example: "And God said . . . . and there was . . ." God spoke a word, and that word became a thing (see Gen. 1:3).

HAGAH: *Hagah* is the Hebrew word that describes the sound of a lion roaring over its caught prey. In fact, like many Hebrew words, *hagah* is an onomatopoeia—it sounds like what it describes. Funny, then, that of several words available to the author of Psalm 1, he decided upon *hagah* to describe a way of poring over God's Torah. Most translators use the word "meditate" as the best choice. Unfortunately, when we think of "meditate," many of us envision a monk with legs crossed on a lonely mountain. For the author of Psalm 1:2, however, the vision of studying God's Word day and night is more like a lion roaring over its prey. You're so hungry, and you cannot get enough![7]

HA-MAN/MANHUE: Translated today as "manna," *ha-man* (also transliterated as *manhue*) originally was a question the Israelites asked when they first saw a flakey substance like frost covering the ground. They said, "*Manhue*?" "What is it?" And so, *ha-man* is how it came to be called. God provided this substance for the Israelites every single day during their forty years in the wilderness, and this remembered provision came to be known as "daily bread" by the first century.[8]

HAVER (PL. HAVERIM): Literally meaning "friend" or "companion," *haver* in the first century was a study partner and fellow disciple—someone you could ask hard questions of and expect hard questions from in return. *Haverim* pushed each other, sometimes to the brink, in order to get to the truth. Calling someone your *haver* also implied that they followed Torah in a similar fashion as you, maybe even following the same rabbi. You would spend the majority of your days with these *haverim* discussing what was most important in your life and the lives of those around you.[9]

KANAF (PL. KANAFAYIM): *Kanaf* in English means "corner." When God commanded the Israelites to wear tassels, He instructed the people to place these tassels on the corners of their garments. *Kanaf* also translates as "wing," as we see in Isaiah 6:2 where the seraphim each having six wings.[10]

L'CHAIM: A traditional Hebrew toast similar to "Cheers!" in English, *L'chaim* simply means "to life!"[11]

MAYIM CHAYIM: Because ritual purification was extremely important for Jews in the first century, they had a lot of conversations a lot about strategies to keep oneself pure. As part of that important topic, the sages discussed the right kind of water to use, not only for purity laws but also for basic hygiene and living. *Mayim chayim* means "living water," and it refers to water that remains moving, not stagnant. Sources for living water include rain, springs, wells, streams, rivers, and freshwater lakes. Basically, any water source that is not carried by human hands or stored in cisterns but comes directly from God Himself is considered *mayim chayim*.[12]

This imagery shows up all over the Old Testament as an image for God, and especially in the New Testament Book of John. Jesus speaks of living water both in John 4 and John 7, where He metaphorically speaks of the Holy Spirit. We see, then, that living water served not only a ritualistic and hygienic purpose, but also a religious and metaphorical purpose. For a people who found themselves in the desert more often than not, few things were more precious or more powerful than the imagery and actuality of *mayim chayim*, living water!

MIKVEH (PL. MIKVE'OT): Beginning in earnest in the first century BC and proceeding to this day, ritual purification (or *mikveh*) has served many purposes throughout the centuries. The forebearer of Christian baptism, *mikve'ot* were stepped immersion pools.[13] An individual would enter the *mikveh* naked, fully submerge themselves, and upon exiting the waters be rendered ritually pure. At least two witnesses had to be present to confirm full immersion.[14] (Because of the emphasis on modesty in Middle Eastern culture, men and women would submerge themselves separately.) The archaeological evidence shows hundreds of these pools. The ruins of these pools serve as a defacto map showing the extent of first century BC and AD Jewish populations and influence—especially in the modern-day states of Israel and Jordan.[15]

MISHNAH: When God gave His Torah to Moses at Mount Sinai, Jews believe He also gave a second set of laws called *Mishnah*, "that which is repeated."[16] The written Torah (or *Mikra*) was far greater in importance, and the oral Torah (or *Mishnah*) expanded and explained what was meant in the written Torah. The *Mishnah* itself explains how it came into existence: "Moses received the Torah at Sinai and transmitted it to Joshua, Joshua to the elders, and the elders to the prophets, and the prophets to the men of the Great Assembly" (*Pirkei Avot 1:1*).[17] From the Great Assembly, that tradition of interpretation carried on through the sages of the first centuries BC and AD, many of whom are called rabbis ("my great ones").[18]

By the beginning of the third century AD it became necessary to write the traditions that had been handed down to that point, a project spearheaded by a man known as Yehudah ha-Nasi, or in English Judah the Prince.[19] This written document offers a small window into Judaism from as early as 300 BC to as late as approximately AD 200.[20] It's divided into six main sections and seven to twelve subsections, starting with the longest and ending with the shortest.[21] Interestingly, the early church organized Paul's letters in the same way in the Bible—longest to shortest.[22]

MISHPAT: Translated most often as "justice" from the Hebrew, *mishpat* serves a special function in the economy of God. Since God advocates for the poor and the oppressed, especially widows and orphans, He expects His followers to do the same. At its core, *mishpat* isn't so much concerned with innocence and guilt as much as honor and shame. To bring justice to the world, God exalts the humble by raising their honor and covering their shame.

Tied closely to another word, *tzedakah*, *mishpat* deals with punishment for wrongdoing, but it is also concerned with equal rights for all—rich and poor, female and male, foreigner and native born. We see a good example of *mishpat* in Numbers 27:1-11 with a tribal land dispute involving a man named Zelophehad who had five daughters and no sons. Strictly because of their gender, the daughters were excluded from any inheritance, but once their case came before Moses, God granted their request and gave them land. This is how *mishpat* works: God raised the daughters' honor by treating them equally—even in a patriarchal society. Ultimately, *mishpat* concerns giving everyone what is due them, whether that is protection, provision, or punishment.[23]

MOUNT GERIZIM: Second in height only to its neighbor Mount Ebal, Mount Gerizim serves as the most sacred location for Samaritans (who still live there to this day). In approximately 128 BC, Jews destroyed the Samaritan temple and attempted to force conversion on all people groups living in the land, including the Samaritans.[24] Needless to say, this attack enlivened the Samaritans to such a degree that animosity on both sides peaked in the first centuries BC and AD.

Mt. Gerizim overshadows the New Testament town of Sychar and specifically Jacob's well.[25] Because of its proximity, the site figures prominently in the conversations Jesus had with the Samaritan woman in John 4.[26]

PARASHAH (PL. PARASHOT): Because the Torah held the primary place within all of Scripture, after the exile, Jews decided to have all five books read aloud throughout the course of a year. In order to accomplish this, they divided the Torah into fifty-four *parashot*, or sections, allowing for one section of a book to be read at the same time every year. Thus, every week a new section of Scripture was studied all week and read aloud in the synagogue for Sabbath.

Literary evidence for this practice occurs not only in the Dead Sea Scrolls, but also in the New Testament. In Luke 4 Jesus follows up the Torah reading with a passage from Isaiah, and in Acts 15, the Jerusalem Council mentions how the Torah was being read in the synagogues every single week.[27]

RABBI ELIEZER: Living at the turn of the first and second centuries AD, Rabbi Eliezer is one of the most quoted sages in the *Mishnah*. He unfortunately made a name for himself through his disagreements with his fellow sages and his more conservative approach to Scripture, eventually being expelled from the Sanhedrin because of a view regarding the usability of a specific kind of oven.[28]

SCHOOLS OF HILLEL AND SHAMMAI: Though very diverse, Pharisaic Judaism in the first centuries BC and AD was ultimately held together and led by two men, Rabbi Hillel[29] and Rabbi Shammai,[30] along with their disciples. Both centered in Jerusalem. Hillel, who lived from approximately 110 BC to AD 10, took a more generous and lenient approach to Scripture. On the other hand, Shammai, who lived from approximately 50 BC to AD 30 took a far more conservative and stern view.

To highlight their differences, a story is told about a student who desired to learn Torah while standing on one foot. When he went to Shammai to inquire how to do this, Shammai beat him with a stick and drove him away, inferring rather violently that it takes a lifetime to master Torah, and it is prideful and insolent to believe one could memorize it while standing on one foot. When the young man went to Hillel and asked the same question, Hillel replied, "What is hateful to you, don't do to others. This is the whole of Torah; the rest is the explanation. Now, go and learn it" (*Shabbat 31a*).[31]

Known for how they disagreed with one another, they were almost always shown in rabbinic literature together, but with opposing arguments. Their differences centered on how to interpret Torah for the culture in which they lived. For example, the question arose as to how one should light the candles for Hanukkah; should you light all eight the first night and subsequently light one less candle for each remaining night? Or should you light one the first night and add to it for the remaining nights? Shammai said the light slowly dwindles through the holiday, while Hillel said it grew (*Shabbat 21b:5*).[32] As was the case in most matters, Hillel's way was followed and not Shammai's. Amazingly, Jesus entered into their debates as well, and in every argument (with the exception of divorce) Jesus favored Hillel's interpretation as opposed to Shammai's.[33]

SEPTUAGINT: A Greek translation of the Hebrew Bible. Greek speaking Jews used the Septuagint (often abbreviated "LXX") as their main text. The early Christians used this translation primarily, which is why Paul quotes from it so often. The history of how the Jewish people came to have this translation is shrouded in myth and mystery, but scholars date the translation to the third to second century BC when a ruler named Ptolemy II invited seventy-two Jewish scholars to Egypt.[34] The story goes that when they arrived, these seventy-two Jewish leaders were placed in seventy-two rooms, where they were each asked to translate the Hebrew Scriptures into Greek, so that future Greek-speaking generations wouldn't lose the Word of God. Hence, the Latin word for "seventy," Septuagint.[35]

TALLIT (PL. TALLITOT): Used to cover the head during prayer, the *tallit* is best translated as a *prayer shawl*. *Tallitot* come in different sizes and colors, but they traditionally extend to arm's length on both sides and can be wrapped around a person like a shawl. Significantly, the corners of the *tallit* represent wings, and symbolically the wings of God serve as a covering for the one praying.[36]

TALMUD (JERUSALEM AND BABYLONIAN): After the *Mishnah* was written down at the beginning of the third century AD, over the next few hundred years, scribes and teachers contributed further commentaries on the written text. That collection of work came to be known as the *Gemara*. As two large centers of learning developed within Judaism—one in Galilee and one in Babylon—these two academies put together the *Mishnah* and *Gemara* into one work known as the *Talmud*. The school in Galilee (Tiberias, specifically) was known as the *Jerusalem Talmud*, while the school in Babylon became known as the *Babylonian Talmud*. Composed in the fourth and fifth centuries AD, respectively, the *Babylonian Talmud* became the more authoritative work.

Perhaps the simplest way to think of these Jewish works is to understand that the Torah is central and most important in all matters of life. The *Mishnah* functions somewhat as a commentary on the Torah, and the *Talmud* serves as a commentary on the *Mishnah*. If a person were to venture off into a school (*yeshiva*) today, they would discover that not only are students studying and memorizing the Torah, they are also studying and memorizing the *Talmud*.

A story is told about a recent scholar in Jerusalem who one day showed up with the entire *Babylonian Talmud* in hand. (Understand, this would be like carrying all the volumes of the *Encyclopedia Britannica* around with you.) Upon entering the classroom, he found one of his prize students and said, "I have committed this to memory. You now go and do the same."[37]

TANAKH (HEBREW BIBLE): What Christians call the Old Testament, Jews call the *Tanakh* or *Mikra* ("that which is called out/read"). Just as we Christians have subdivided the Old Testament into categories (i.e., Law, History, Poetry, Major Prophets, and Minor Prophets), so too have the Jews. The letters T, N, and K come from the first letter of those three sections of Scripture for the Jew: Torah (Instruction or Law), *Nevi'im* (Prophets), and *Ketuvim* (Writings).[38]

The weight of authority given to these sections, however, is another matter. For the Jew, nothing is more important than Torah. The Torah is the first place they go when deriving authority from Scripture. The books of Torah include Genesis, Exodus, Leviticus, Numbers, and Deuteronomy, what scholars today call the Pentateuch ("five books"). Though traditionally translated as "law," the word Torah implies instruction more than law.[39] The Jewish people carry the idea that the commandments offer freedom more than oppression. The commandments are parameters that allow a person to function well in their family, tribe, and nation.

The second section, the Prophets, functions almost like a commentary on the Torah, offering interpretations and examples of what to do and what not to do within the system of laws God has set up. The books of the Hebrew Bible within this section include: Joshua, Judges, 1 and 2 Samuel, 1 and 2 Kings, Isaiah, Jeremiah, Ezekiel, Hosea, Joel, Amos, Obadiah, Jonah, Micah, Nahum, Habakkuk, Zephaniah, Haggai, Zechariah, and Malachi.

The third section, the Writings, is considered the least authoritative, but is still considered God's Word and part of the Bible. The books include: Psalms, Proverbs, Job, Song of Songs, Ruth, Lamentations, Ecclesiastes, Esther, Daniel, Ezra, Nehemiah, and 1 and 2 Chronicles.[40]

The books of the Hebrew Bible, though reckoned differently than ours and in a different order, offer the same content. In the Hebrew Bible, the books fall relatively in the order in which they were written. This leads us to a fascinating theological insight: The entirety of the Hebrew Bible begins and ends in a similar place. *Tanakh* starts with Genesis and finishes with Chronicles, theologically driving an exiled people back to Jerusalem and its environs—in essence, to a new Eden. Thus, what begins in Genesis in a garden (the garden of Eden), ends in Chronicles with a desire and call to return to a new "Eden," the land of Israel, with Jerusalem as its epicenter.

The order we find the books within the Christian Old Testament also points to a new reality. God speaks, and physical existence comes to be; God's Word is made flesh. By ending our Old Testament with Malachi, we look with anticipation not to a place, but to a person. Thus, we see how God's Word was made flesh not only in the creation of the universe, but also in the bringing forth of the Son—Jesus—who was and is the perfect manifestation of God. "The Word became flesh and made His dwelling among us" (John 1:14).

TEKHELET: The *tekhelet* is the blue cord in each *tzitzit*. Because the memory of the precise dying process has been lost, Orthodox Jews today very rarely incorporate the blue dye in a tassel. Through archaeological discoveries, however, scholars have identified the Murex snail as the most likely producer of the blue color needed, and as further research takes place, perhaps the dying process will be reinstated.[41]

TZEDAKAH: *Tzedakah* means "righteousness" and so much more. Placed within the realm of relationships, *tzedakah* serves to make things right, and it does so through generosity. Another translation of the Hebrew word could easily be mercy.[42] In fact, an act of righteousness in the first century was giving to the poor. (See Matt. 6:1-4.) By not sharing with others, one violates the very justice, will, and command of God. This practice reveals that *tzedakah* is not optional in God's economy.

When coupled with *mishpat*, as is the case dozens of times in the Old Testament, we can clearly see the character of God Himself. We first see these words together in Genesis 18:19 when God says of Abraham: "For I have chosen him, so that he will direct his children and his household after him to keep the way of the LORD by doing what is *right* and *just*, so that the LORD will bring about for Abraham what he has promised him" (emphasis added). As evidenced in this passage, the way of the Lord is practicing both *mishpat* and *tzedakah* together—a generous lifting up.

TZITZIT (PL. TZITZIYOT): In Numbers 15:37-40, God commanded the Israelites to wear tassels on the corners of their garments. The *tzitzit* or tassel reminded the wearer of God's commandments in order that they might be obeyed.[43] So important was the passage of Scripture that to this day it is recited after the *Shema* in Jewish prayers. The significance of how and where the tassels were to be tied and worn grew just before and after the destruction of the temple, and Jesus, as a religious Jew, would have worn *tzitziyot* on His garments. Jesus actually referred to tassels in Matthew 23:5 in His criticism of hypocritical Pharisees who tried to make theirs extra long.

The Greek term used for tassels in the Old Testament is *kraspedon*, meaning "corner" or "hem." It's the same Greek term used when the woman with the "issue of blood" grabbed the hem of Jesus's garment.[44]

Today, *tzitziyot* are carefully tied so that every knot and space carry meaning (in other words, five knots represent the five Books of Moses [Torah], and four spaces between the knots represent the four letters in God's sacred name, *YHWH*).[45]

YESHIVA: Today, *yeshiva* is a formal term referring to an established educational system focused on studying the Torah and the *Talmud*. In the first century, however, the emphasis on the term lay in how a teacher interpreted a specific passage of Scripture or theological concept and if that teaching was valid. How would a community determine validity? *Yeshiva*.

Yeshiva occurred constantly as students would debate questions or comments from a teacher. They were "sitting in" the concept, so to speak—arguing and debating among themselves whether or not what the teacher communicated should be implemented into daily life and how it could be done. Learning occurred in a multidimensional way as arguments among peers and teachers were raised and discussed. In this line of thinking, the better a community knows the Bible, the more profound the insights as other passages and teachers' interpretations are brought in to bear on the topic.[46]

ZAKHAR: Occurring more than 230 times in the Old Testament alone, *zakhar* means "remembered."[47] It appears more than one hundred times in the positive form, "do not forget." When God speaks to His people, especially through prophets like Moses, remembrance is a repeated theme. One of the ways that Jews in the first century took God's words to heart was by repeating their lessons over and over again. In the *Babylonian Talmud* we read these words from Hillel (who lived in the first century BC): "One who reviews his studies one hundred times is not comparable to the one who reviews his studies one hundred and one times" (*Chagigah 9b*).[48] In other words, repetition solidifies learning and is key to remembrance.

ENDNOTES

INTRODUCTION

1. Russell Moore, "If you hate Jews, you hate Jesus," *The Washington Post*, Oct. 31, 2018, accessed Oct. 21, 2019, https://www.washingtonpost.com/religion/2018/10/29/christian-message-about-pittsburgh-synagogue-shooting-if-you-hate-jews-you-hate-jesus-too/.
2. Gary M. Burge, *Jesus, the Middle Eastern Storyteller* (Grand Rapids, MI: Zondervan, 2009), 11.

SESSION ONE

1. Rabbi Yissachar Dov Rubin, *Talelei Oros—The Holiday Anthology* (Jerusalem: Feldheim Publishers, 2003), 207.
2. John D. Garr, *Life From the Dead: The Dynamic Saga of the Chosen People* (Atlanta: Hebraic Christian Global Community, 2015), 31-34.

SESSION TWO

1. *Merriam-Webster*, s.v. "Tallit," accessed October 7, 2019, https://www.merriam-webster.com/dictionary/tallit.
2. Merriam-Webster, s.v. "Tzitzit," accessed October 7, 2019, https://www.merriam-webster.com/dictionary/tzitzit.
3. Rabbi Abraham Millgram, "The Tallit: Spiritual Significance," *My Jewish Learning*, accessed Oct. 22, 2019, https://www.myjewishlearning.com/article/the-tallit-spiritual-significance/.
4. Strong's H3671, *Blue Letter Bible*, accessed Sept. 30, 2019, https://www.blueletterbible.org/lang/lexicon/lexicon.cfm?strongs=H3671.
5. Noga Tarnopolsky, "The Bible described it as the perfect, pure blue. And then for nearly 2,000 years, everyone forgot what it looked like," *Los Angeles Times*, Sept. 10, 2018, accessed Oct. 7, 2019, https://www.latimes.com/world/la-fg-israel-blue-20180910-htmlstory.html.
6. *Encyclopedia Britannica*, ed. Brian Duignan, s.v. "Torah, Sacred Text," Sept. 18, 2019, accessed Oct. 7, 2019, https://www.britannica.com/topic/Torah.
7. Herbert Lockyer, *All the Women of the Bible* (Grand Rapids, MI: Zondervan Publishing House, 1988), 221.
8. Strong's G2899, *Blue Letter Bible*, accessed Oct. 7, 2019, https://www.blueletterbible.org/lang/lexicon/lexicon.cfm?t=kjv&strongs=g2899.
9. Kent Dobson, *NIV First Century Study Bible* (Grand Rapids, MI: Zondervan, 2014), 1,208.
10. Strong's H1697, *Blue Letter Bible*, accessed September 30, 2019, https://www.blueletterbible.org/lang/lexicon/lexicon.cfm?strongs=H1697.

SESSION THREE

1. Strong's H4941, *Blue Letter Bible*, accessed September 30, 2019, https://www.blueletterbible.org/lang/lexicon/lexicon.cfm?strongs=H4941.
2. Strong's H6666, *Blue Letter Bible*, accessed September 30, 2019, https://www.blueletterbible.org/lang/lexicon/lexicon.cfm?strongs=H6666.
3. Gregory the Great, *Commentary on the Book of Blessed Job*, accessed September 26, 2019, http://faculty.georgetown.edu/jod/texts/moralia1.html.
4. Gerald L. Baum, MD, "L'Chaim!" *JAMA Internal Medicine, Arch Intern Med.*, (August 1979): 921, accessed September 30, 2019, doi:10.1001/archinte.1979.03630450063021.
5. Strong's H1004, *Blue Letter Bible*, accessed October 8, 2019, https://www.blueletterbible.org/lang/lexicon/lexicon.cfm?strongs=H1004.
6. *Mishnah Middot 1:3, Sefaria*, accessed Nov. 26, 2019, https://www.sefaria.org/Mishnah_Middot.1?lang=bi.
7. *Encyclopedia Britannica*, eds., s.v. "Mishna," accessed Dec. 2, 2019, https://www.britannica.com/topic/Mishna.
8. *Encyclopedia Britannica*, Encyclopedia Britannica, eds., s.v. "Judah ha-Nasi," accessed Oct. 8, 2019, https://www.britannica.com/biography/Judah-ha-Nasi.
9. J. E. Bechman, Luis Colina, Hagal Netzer, eds., *The Nearest Active Galaxies* (Dordrecht, Netherlands: Springer Science+Business Media, 1993), 279.
10. Jacob Neusner, ed., *A History of the Mishnaic Law of Purities, Part 15: Niddah: Commentary,* (Eugene, OR: Wipf and Stock Publishers, 1976), I.
11. "14 The Southern Steps and Psalms of Ascent Reminders," *Bible.org*, accessed Oct. 30, 2019, https://bible.org/seriespage/14-southern-steps-and-psalms-ascent-reminders.
12. David Wright, "How Long Were the Israelites in Egypt?", *Answers in Genesis*, July 5, 2010, accessed Oct. 30, 2019, https://answersingenesis.org/bible-questions/how-long-were-the-israelites-in-egypt/.

13. Walter Brueggemann, "The Liturgy of Abundance, the Myth of Scarcity: Consumerism and Religious Life," *Christian Century,* March 24-31, 1999, accessed Nov. 26, 2019, http://therivardreport.com/wp-content/uploads/2016/09/the_liturgy_of_abundance.pdf.

SESSION FOUR

1. Charles J. Ellicott, *Elicott's Commentary for English Readers, Vol. 3, John 4:4* (USA: Delmarva Publications, Inc., 2015).
2. Elinoar Bareket, "The Evolution of Biblical Terms through the Ages," *Achva Academic College,* October 2017, Vol. 7, No. 10, 543-552, accessed Oct. 23, 2019, doi: 10.17265/2159-5313/2017.10.004.
3. Strong's H1897, *Blue Letter Bible,* accessed September 30, 2019, https://www.blueletterbible.org/lang/lexicon/lexicon.cfm?t=kjv&strongs=h1897.
4. *God Heard Their Cry Discovery Guide* (Grand Rapids, MI: Zondervan, 2009).
5. J.W. McGarvey and Philip Y. Pendleton, *The Fourfold Gospel,* "At Jacob's Well, and at Sychar," via *Bible Study Tools,* accessed Oct. 30, 2019, https://www.biblestudytools.com/commentaries/the-fourfold-gospel/by-sections/at-jacobs-well-and-at-sychar.html.
6. "Mount Gerizim," *Jewish Virtual Library,* accessed Oct. 30, 2019, https://www.jewishvirtuallibrary.org/gerizim-mount.
7. Judah Goldin, *Encyclopedia Britannica,* s.v. "Hillel," accessed Oct. 29, 2019, https://www.britannica.com/biography/Hillel.
8. *Encyclopedia Britannica,* s.v. "Shammai ha-Zaken," accessed Oct. 29, 2019, https://www.britannica.com/biography/Shammai-ha-Zaken.
9. "Hillel and Shammai," *Jewish Virtual Library: American-Israeli Cooperative Enterprise,* accessed September 26, 2019, https://www.jewishvirtuallibrary.org/hillel-and-shammai.
10. David L. Turner and Darrell L. Bock, *The Gospel of Matthew – The Gospel of Mark* (Carol Stream: IL, Tyndale House Publishers, 2005), 246.
11. "*Gittin 90a-b: Grounds for Divorce,*" Aleph Society Inc., 2018, accessed September 30, 2019, https://steinsaltz.org/daf/gittin90/.
12. Ibid.
13. Joachim Jeremias, *Jerusalem in the Time of Jesus,* trans. F.H. and C.H. Cave, (USA: SCM Press, 1969), 370.
14. Ibid.

SESSION FIVE

1. Merriam-Webster, s.v. "Parashah," accessed Oct. 23, 2019, https://www.merriam-webster.com/dictionary/parashah.
2. David M. Morgan, ed., *The Weekly Torah Portion: A One-Year Journey Through the Parasha Readings,* (Lake Mary, FL: Charisma House Book Group, 2019).
3. MJL, MJL Admin, "What is the Torah portion?" *My Jewish Learning,* accessed Oct. 30, 2019, https://www.myjewishlearning.com/article/what-is-the-torah-portion/.
4. Merriam-Webster, s.v. "Parashah," accessed Oct. 23, 2019, https://www.merriam-webster.com/dictionary/parashah.
5. Paul Anthony Chilton, Monika Weronika Kopytowska, eds., *Religion, Language, and the Human Mind,* (New York: Oxford University Press, 2018), 311.
6. Walter Brueggemann, *From Whom No Secrets Are Hid: Introducing the Psalms* (Louisville, KY: Westminster John Knox Press, 2014), xxiii.
7. Merriam-Webster, s.v. "Homo mensura," accessed Oct. 15, 2019, https://www.merriam-webster.com/dictionary/homo%20mensura.
8. Strong's H1980, *Blue Letter Bible,* accessed Oct. 15, 2019, https://www.blueletterbible.org/lang/lexicon/lexicon.cfm?strongs=H1980.

SESSION SIX

1. Brad H. Young, *The Parables: Jewish Tradition and Christian Interpretation* (Grand Rapids: MI, Baker Academic, 1998), 37.
2. Kenneth E. Bailey, *Finding the Lost* (St. Louis: Concordian, 1992), 97-99.
3. *Merriam-Webster,* s.v. "Chutzpah," accessed Oct. 16, 2019, https://www.merriam-webster.com/dictionary/chutzpah.
4. Strong's H2142, *Blue Letter Bible,* accessed September 30, 2019, https://www.blueletterbible.org/lang/lexicon/lexicon.cfm?t=kjv&strongs=h2142.
5. Don Stewart, "Why is the Bible Divided into Chapters and Verses?", *Blue Letter Bible,* accessed Oct. 25, 2019, https://www.blueletterbible.org/faq/don_stewart/don_stewart_273.cfm.

6. Kenneth Bailey, *The Cross and the Prodigal: Luke 15 Through the Eyes of Middle Eastern Peasants* (Downers Grove, IL: InterVarsity Press, 2005), 34.
7. N.T. Wright, *Luke for Everyone* (London: Society for Promoting Christian Knowledge, 2001), 187.

SESSION SEVEN

1. Richard E. Creel, *The Love of Jesus: The Heart of Christianity* (Eugene: OR, Resource Publications, 2010), 26.
2. Wayne Stiles, "The Southern Steps and the songs of the High Holidays,"*The Jerusalem Post*, Sept. 19, 2011, accessed Oct. 21, 2019, https://www.jpost.com/Travel/Jerusalem/The-Southern-Steps-and-the-songs-of-the-High-Holidays.
3. Strong's H8527, *Blue Letter Bible*, accessed Oct. 21, 2019, https://www.blueletterbible.org/lang/lexicon/lexicon.cfm?t=kjv&strongs=h8527.
4. "Being a first century disciple," Bible.org, accessed Oct. 25, 2019, https://bible.org/article/being-first-century-disciple.
5. Earl D. Radmacher, ed., *Nelson's New Illustrated Bible Commentary*, (Nashville, TN: Thomas Nelson, 1999), 1787.
6. Thomas L. Friedman, *From Beirut to Jerusalem* (New York: Picador, 2012), 429.
7. Strong's G266, *Blue Letter Bible*, accessed Oct. 22, 2019, https://www.blueletterbible.org/lang/lexicon/lexicon.cfm?t=kjv&strongs=g266.
8. Strong's H3384, *Blue Letter Bible*, accessed Oct. 21, 2019, https://www.blueletterbible.org/lang/lexicon/lexicon.cfm?t=kjv&strongs=h3384.
9. Strong's H7965, *Blue Letter Bible*, accessed Oct. 22, 2019, https://www.blueletterbible.org/lang/lexicon/lexicon.cfm?t=kjv&strongs=h7965.
10. Susan Schreiner, *Are You Alone Wise?: The Search For Certainty in the Early Modern Era* (New York: Oxford University Press, 2011), 159.

SESSION EIGHT

1. Deidre Joy Good, ed., *Mariam, the Magdalen, and the Mother,* (Bloomington, IN: Indiana University Press, 2005), 12.
2. "Miriam," *Jewish Virtual Library*, accessed Oct. 30, 2019, https://www.jewishvirtuallibrary.org/miriam.
3. "Mary," *Behind the Name*, accessed September 25, 2019, https://www.behindthename.com/name/mary.
4. "Miriam," *Behind the Name*, accessed Oct. 24, 2019, https://www.behindthename.com/name/miriam.

GLOSSARY

1. James Orr, ed., *International Standard Bible Encyclopedia*, Bible Study Tools, s.v. "Sirach, Book Of," accessed September 30, 2019, https://www.biblestudytools.com/encyclopedias/isbe/sirach-book-of.html.
2. Ibid.
3. Manning Jr., https://www.biola.edu/blogs/good-book-blog/2011/good-eye-bad-eye.
4. A. Vanlier Hunter, *Biblical Hebrew Workbook* (Lanham, MD: University Press of America, 1988), 69.
5. James Orr, ed., *International Standard Bible Encyclopedia*, Bible Study Tools, s.v. "Stiff-Necked" accessed September 30, 2019, https://www.biblestudytools.com/encyclopedias/isbe/stiff-necked.html.
6. Strong's H1697, *Blue Letter Bible*, accessed September 30, 2019, https://www.blueletterbible.org/lang/lexicon/lexicon.cfm?strongs=H1697.
7. Strong's H1897, *Blue Letter Bible*, accessed September 30, 2019. https://www.blueletterbible.org/lang/lexicon/lexicon.cfm?strongs=H1897.
8. Brueggemann, http://therivardreport.com/wp-content/uploads/2016/09/the_liturgy_of_abundance.pdf.
9. Bareket, "The Evolution of Biblical Terms through the Ages," 543-552, doi: 10.17265/2159-5313/2017.10.004.
10. Strong's H3671, *Blue Letter Bible*, accessed September 30, 2019, https://www.blueletterbible.org/lang/lexicon/lexicon.cfm?strongs=H3671.
11. Baum, 921, doi:10.1001/archinte.1979.03630450063021.
12. Garr, *Life from the Dead: The Dynamic Saga of the Chosen People,* 31-34.
13. MJL, "Why Some Jewish Women Go to the Mikveh Each Month," *My Jewish Learning,* accessed Oct. 29, 2019, https://www.myjewishlearning.com/article/the-laws-of-niddah-taharat-hamishpaha/.
14. Susan Freudenheim, "Becoming Jewish: Tales from the Mikveh," *Jewish Journal,* May 8, 2013, accessed Oct. 29, 2019, https://jewishjournal.com/cover_story/116511/.
15. Jerzy Gawronski and Ranjith Jayasena, "A mid-18th century mikveh unearthed in the Jewish Historical Museum in Amsterdam," *Taylor and Francis Online*, July 19, 2013, accessed Oct. 24, 2019, 213-221, https://www.tandfonline.com/doi/abs/10.1179/174581307X318985.

16. Encyclopedia Britannica, Encyclopedia Britannica, eds., s.v. "Mishna," accessed Dec. 2, 2019, https://www.britannica.com/topic/Mishna.

17. *Pirkei Avot 1:1, Sefaria*, accessed Oct. 29, 2019, https://www.sefaria.org/Pirkei_Avot.1?lang=bi.

18. Strong's G4461, *Blue Letter Bible*, accessed Oct. 29, 2019, https://www.blueletterbible.org/lang/lexicon/lexicon.cfm?t=kjv&strongs=g4461.

19. Nissan HaNasi, "Rabbi Judah the Prince," *Kehot Publication Society,* accessed Oct. 29, 2019, https://www.chabad.org/library/article_cdo/aid/112279/jewish/Rabbi-Judah-the-Prince.htm.

20. J. E. Bechman, Luis Colina, Hagal Netzer, eds.,*The Nearest Active Galaxies*, 279.

21. *A History of the Mishnaic Law of Purities, Part 15: Niddah: Commentary,* Jacob Neusner, ed. (Eugene, OR: Wipf and Stock Publishers, 1976), I.

22. Daniel Lynwood Smith, *Into the World of the New Testament* (London: Bloomsbury T&T Clark, 2015), 8.

23. Strong's H4941, *Blue Letter Bible*, accessed Dec. 2, 2019, https://www.blueletterbible.org/lang/lexicon/lexicon.cfm?t=kjv&strongs=h4941.

24. Bailey, *Jesus Through Middle Eastern Eyes*, 203.

25. "At Jacob's Well, and at Sychar," *Bible Study Tools*, accessed Oct. 29, 2019, https://www.biblestudytools.com/commentaries/the-fourfold-gospel/by-sections/at-jacobs-well-and-at-sychar.html.

26. *Encyclopedia Britannica*, s.v. "Mount Gerizim," Encyclopedia Britannica, eds., accessed September 30, 2019, https://www.britannica.com/place/Mount-Gerizim.

27. *Merriam-Webster*, s.v. "Parashah," accessed Oct. 23, 2019, https://www.merriam-webster.com/dictionary/parashah.

28. Charlotte Elisheva Fonrobert, "When the Rabbi Weeps: On Reading Gender in Talmudic Aggadah." *Nashim: A Journal of Jewish Women's Studies & Gender Issues 4* (2001): 56-83, https://www.muse.jhu.edu/article/409419.

29. Judah Goldin, *Encyclopedia Britannica*, s.v. "Hillel," accessed Oct. 29, 2019, https://www.britannica.com/biography/Hillel.

30. *Encyclopedia Britannica*, s.v. "Shammai ha-Zaken," accessed Oct. 29, 2019, https://www.britannica.com/biography/Shammai-ha-Zaken.

31. *Shabbat 31a, Sefaria*, accessed Oct. 30, 2019, https://www.sefaria.org/Shabbat.31a?lang=bi.

32. *Shabbat 21b:5, Sefaria*, accessed Oct. 30, 2019, https://www.sefaria.org/sheets/89557?lang=bi.

33. Michael Card, *Matthew: The Gospel of Identity* (Downers Grove, IL: InterVarsity Press, 2013), 170.

34. Malka Z. Simkovich, *Discovering Second Temple Literature* (Lincoln: University of Nebraska Press, 2018), 108.

35. *Encyclopedia Britannica*, s.v. "Septuagint," accessed Oct. 29, 2019, https://www.britannica.com/topic/Septuagint.

36. Merriam-Webster, s.v. "Tallit," accessed September 30, 2019, https://www.merriam-webster.com/dictionary/tallit.

37. Rabbi Jill Jacobs, "Tale of Two Talmuds: Jerusalem and Babylonian," *My Jewish Learning*, accessed Oct. 29, 2019, ttps://www.myjewishlearning.com/article/tale-of-two-talmuds/.

38. Patrick T. Brown, *Embracing Biblical Literacy* (Bloomington, IN: WestBow Press, 2019).

39. Strong's H8451, *Blue Letter Bible*, accessed Oct. 29, 2019, https://www.blueletterbible.org/lang/lexicon/lexicon.cfm?t=kjv&strongs=h8451.

40. "The Tanakh," *Jewish Virtual Library*, accessed Oct. 29, 2019, https://www.jewishvirtuallibrary.org/the-tanakh.

41. Tarnopolsky, "The Bible described it as the perfect, pure blue. And then for nearly 2,000 years, everyone forgot what it looked like," https://www.latimes.com/world/la-fg-israel-blue-20180910-htmlstory.html#.

42. Strong's H6666, *Blue Letter Bible*, accessed Oct. 29, 2019, https://www.blueletterbible.org/lang/lexicon/lexicon.cfm?strongs=H6666.

43. *Merriam-Webster*, s.v. "Tzitzit," accessed September 30, 2019, https://www.merriam-webster.com/dictionary/tzitzit.

44. Pinchas Shir, "The Fringe of His Garment," *Israel Bible Center*, March 28, 2018, accessed Oct. 30, 2019, https://weekly.israelbiblecenter.com/the-fringe-of-his-garment/.

45. Craig Wagganer, *Simple Lessons Learned Along the Way* (Bloomington, IN: WestBow Press, 2015).

46. *Merriam-Webster*, s.v. "Yeshiva," accessed September 30, 2019, https://www.merriam-webster.com/dictionary/yeshiva.

47. Strong's H2142, *Blue Letter Bible*, accessed September 30, 2019, https://www.blueletterbible.org/lang/lexicon/lexicon.cfm?t=kjv&strongs=h2142.

48. *Chagigah 9b, Sefaria*, accessed Oct. 29, 2019, https://www.sefaria.org/Chagigah.9b?lang=bi.

THE GOSPEL ON THE GROUND
BY KRISTI MCLELLAND

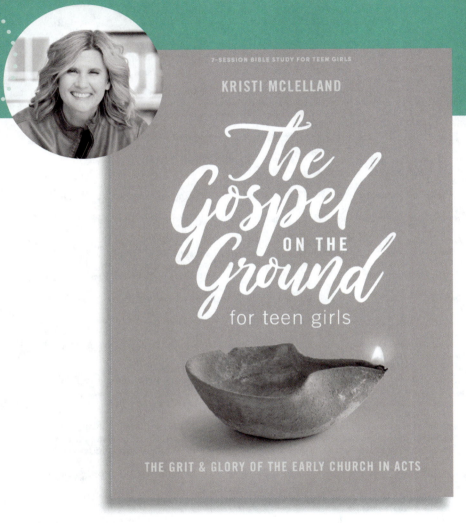

7-SESSION BIBLE STUDY FOR TEEN GIRLS

KRISTI MCLELLAND

The Gospel ON THE Ground for teen girls

THE GRIT & GLORY OF THE EARLY CHURCH IN ACTS

Jesus, for the vast majority of His life, never traveled outside of a one-hundred-mile radius from where He was born. Yet His name is spoken and known in every corner of the earth. This is the story of how that happened. And it's the story of how it is still happening today.

NOTES

NOTES

NOTES

NOTES

NOTES

Get the most from your study.

IN THIS STUDY, YOU'LL:

- Explore how Jesus generously restores dignity and honor to women in the first century and now.
- Gain deeper insight into the biblical world, including fresh perspective on familiar Bible stories.
- Discover the Bible through the lens of Middle Eastern culture.

Kristi's teaching sessions are essential for the learning impact of the study. This Bible study book is written to prepare you for the teachings, not to stand alone. Each session unpacks fundamental truths taught in *Jesus and Women* and clarifies your study time questions.

Watch Kristi McLelland's teaching sessions, available for purchase at lifeway.com/jesusandwomen.

ALSO AVAILABLE

Video teaching bundle:
Includes 8 videos, 15-minutes each from Kristi McLelland

Women's Bible Study book:
Includes one *Jesus and Women* Bible study book for women

Browse companion products, a free session sample, video clips, promotional material, and more at

lifeway.com/jesusandwomen